ENGAGING WITH

Islam

AN EVANGELICAL DOCTRINAL PERSPECTIVE

Ian S McNaughton

DayOne

© Day One Publications 2019
Reprinted 2020

ISBN 978-1-84625-659-2

British Library Cataloguing in Publication Data available

Published by Day One Publications
Ryelands Road, Leominster, HR6 8NZ
Telephone 01568 613 740 FAX 01568 611 473
email—sales@dayone.co.uk
web site—www.dayone.co.uk

Cover design by Kathryn Chedgzoy
Printed by 4Edge

To the saints and faithful in Christ Jesus:
grace to you and peace
from God our Father and the Lord Jesus Christ.

ENDORSEMENTS

How do we as Christians deal with the claims Muslims make? We could simply ignore them, but that could have a negative effect on our witness. What we need in today's climate of increasing Muslim influence upon our society is to understand the issues more clearly—especially to have a greater awareness of biblical truth. Being aware of Muslim thinking through having ministered among Muslims, I have a deep personal concern for Christians to have a better understanding. I have been exercised for many years about the need for such a book as Ian has written, for we need to be equipped to stand up to the opposition we face. Ian asserts in this book, 'If Islam is free to deny and challenge the Christian Scripture's view of its Messiah Jesus Christ and its worldview . . . I reserve the right to challenge Islam's religious views . . . [arguing] for Bible integrity, authority and sufficiency, upholding the view that Jesus Christ is God's last Prophet to the world before the Second Coming and Judgement Day.' Ian examines relevant doctrines, comparing them with Muslim claims and showing how we are to 'embrace the truth as it is in Jesus'. It is my privilege to commend this book to help us understand the issues we face today. I have wished that a book might be written to make Christians aware of the sorts of issues that Muslims attack and how they seek to mislead. It is essential to take notice of the things we believe, and to encourage believers to fully get to grips with the issues.

Edward Challen, retired Baptist pastor, former missionary in Bangladesh and author of Love Your Muslim Neighbour **(Day One, 2018)**

This is a very helpful book for anyone interested in understanding what Muslims believe in comparison with what the Bible teaches. Rev. Ian McNaughton sets out the clear teachings of the historic Christian faith alongside those of Islam. He draws upon a wide range of scholarship, both Muslim and Christian, to demonstrate that Islam is incompatible with Christianity and that it is only through Jesus Christ that we can find forgiveness of sins, peace with God and everlasting life. I highly commend this book.

Paul Barnes, Secretary of Fellowship of Faith for Muslims

I think this is an excellent work. It focuses on main points of conflict and contrast between the truth and Islamic error and how they are totally at odds with one another.

Rev. John W. Keddie, Free Church of Scotland (Continuing) and author

UK evangelicals are increasingly faced with the formidable challenge that Islam is posing to their faith. Wherein lie the differences between biblical Christianity and Islam? Do they matter? How does an evangelical go about witnessing to his or her Muslim friends in a respectful but knowledgeable manner? It is my belief that Ian McNaughton has heavily contributed towards answering these questions. His book is concise and to the point. In a highly readable style, it serves to provide that fundamentally important knowledge that evangelicals need regarding Islam, and which will also help them to be firmly grounded in their witness to their Muslim co-workers and friends. It is a book worth having in one's personal library.

Florenc Mene, PhD student, Edinburgh University, and converted Muslim

The best way to recognize a counterfeit is not to study counterfeits but to study the genuine article. In this very helpful book, Ian McNaughton does just that, boldly affirming the core truths of the Christian faith and then showing how, on every count, Islam falls far short, thus revealing it to be a false religion. This book will both edify believers in 'the faith' and also equip them to recognize and counter falsehood, and not just in Islam.

Rev. John D. Brand, Principal, Edinburgh Bible College

I have known Ian McNaughton for about thirteen years, working with a major apologetics ministry and observing his pastoral work. It is with a pastor's heart that he writes this book, because many of our flocks are increasingly coming into contact with Islam. Islam is presenting two faces to the world: one is the frightening face of public terrorism, but the other is that of a benign alternative to an outmoded Christianity in our societies. Ian systematically tackles the relevant issues one by one. Common Islamic claims about true Christianity—on subjects such as the virgin birth, the deity of Christ, the history of Abraham, and the death and resurrection of Jesus, among others—are examined, and positions in opposition to the Bible are refuted. But Ian does not do this out of a sense of competition but out of a love for those within our orbit who might be attracted to the 'lighter' side of Islam, and also out of love for Muslims themselves, that they may come to know the true Saviour and find that reconciliation with God that is not possible through their own trust in Islam. Pastors will need this book. Parents will need this book. Church members will need this book. Evangelists will need this book. You need this book. That is why I am so pleased to be able heartily to recommend it to you.

Paul Taylor, author, broadcaster, and Director of the Mount St Helens Creation Center, Castle Rock, WA, USA

We all have to engage with Islam—some of us more than others. Ian McNaughton presents a useful overview of the differences between the underlying thinking of Islam and Christianity which every thinking Christian ought to be aware of. Although this book presents arguments in favour of a Christian position, the author has tried to fairly represent the thinking of Islam in a comparative study. The material is laid out in a systematic fashion that makes it easy to refer to. I do think it is necessary for Christian pastors to be well informed about the theological matters at stake, particularly as communities of Islamic tradition interact with Western culture. Anyone who wants to truly understand religious practices must become acquainted with their doctrinal basis. I recommend this book.

ST, missionary in the Muslim world

Islamic influence is sweeping vigorously across Europe and is being welcomed by nearly all government and public bodies. Many people mistakenly think that Islam is very similar to Christianity and poses no threat to a traditional Christian heritage. In this book Ian McNaughton expertly summarizes the teaching of the Quran and the Bible and shows how they are doctrinally radically different and totally incompatible. A very succinct and readable little book which everyone should peruse. I thoroughly enjoyed it and learned a lot.

Dr Robert Beckett, Evangelical Presbyterian Church, Northern Ireland

I found Engaging with Islam *interesting and helpful. It's a little bit like a 'mini systematic theology'—aimed at Christians rather than Muslims—on those areas where Islam and Christianity disagree. Though I knew something of what Islam teaches, there were many other areas of Islamic belief in which my knowledge was quite limited. This book was particularly helpful at those points. It should prove to be of much value to many trying to get to grips with Islamic beliefs and to engage effectively with Muslims.*

Ray Trainer, pastor, Hoylake Evangelical Church

In this book Ian McNaughton takes us through the main Christian doctrines, such as God, His attributes, sin, salvation and the life to come, and compares them with Islamic teaching on the same topics. There is a deliberate emphasis on seeking to explain the Christian teaching from Scripture and then simply and without any hostility show that these great truths are contradicted in the teaching of Islam. I believe this book will be a useful resource for Christians and for those seeking the truth found in Jesus.

Graham Nicholls, Director, Affinity

Contents

W e are not against religious freedom, nor are we against social harmony. As I write this small book my only aim is to spread the truth as it is in Jesus Christ for the glory of God in heaven. I am concerned about the true identity of Jesus Christ and His historical Person.

We respect those Muslims—whether Sunni, Shia or Sufi[1]—who, out of a sincere faith in their religion, possess a fear of God the Almighty and worship Him according to their conscience without violence. However, believing in the infallibility of the Bible, I will endeavour to speak the truth in love about God's way of salvation as it is revealed through the Scriptures, the Old and New Testaments. The Bible is the power and authority behind the rise and success of Christianity for two thousand years and its authority and sufficiency have not diminished with the passing of time or the rise of false religions. Christianity is a supernatural religion given by God to the world through His Son Jesus Christ. It is based on historical realities and special revelation. Around 500 years ago the magisterial Reformer Martin Luther said, 'The Word so greatly weakened the papacy . . . I did nothing; the Word did everything . . . I did nothing; I let the Word do its work.'[2] He was speaking, of course, about the effect and success of the gospel of justification by faith when it was again preached in sixteenth-century Europe after a thousand years of the Papacy and the Dark Ages. We are convinced that it is the anointed proclamation of the gospel that saves us from the wrath to come that will also bring Muslims to Christ in our generation in the will of God.

The cults are still about, though perhaps they are not so active today. But it is the rise of Islam in the West that is the next and greatest challenge to the contemporary Western church. It can no longer ignore Islam as it has done in the past. Islam cannot be restrained by war and ethnic cleansing as it was when Muslims attacked western Europe in the form of the Ottoman Empire (1299–1922). Today, the rise of Islam in the West is a challenge to pastors and church leaders (especially those appointed to teach) as it is their responsibility to prepare their congregations—especially the young among them—for the difficult days ahead for Christianity in the UK and Europe through preaching and teaching about what Islam and Muslims believe.

Is Islam an antichrist? It is time we accepted that Islam's clear rejection of Jesus Christ and His teaching points in that direction. This rejection the Apostle John calls a 'transgression' for not abiding in 'the doctrine of Christ' (2 John 9). Earlier, in his first epistle, John, speaking about the Trinitarian Son of God, also clearly declares, 'Who is a liar but he who denies that Jesus is the Christ? He is antichrist who denies the Father and the Son. Whoever denies the Son does not have the Father either; he who acknowledges the Son has the Father also' (1 John 2:22–23).

Is this book about converting Muslims to Christianity? I would be happy if followers of Islam read and learned from it. However, my primary motivation is to inform Christians and other enquirers about the historic Jesus Christ whom Christians believe is the only Saviour of the world (John 3:16). My emphasis on the Person and Work of Jesus Christ is deliberate as He alone is the Saviour of the world (John 14:6). The sixty-six books of the Bible witness to Christ's unique and unrivalled place in the pantheon of God's prophets, placing Him first and last (Rev. 1:8). Cults, sects and religions which deny the true Person and Work of the historical Jesus place themselves above the biblical revelation and deny its integrity. It is my hope that the incarnate Son of God—the Jesus of history and Saviour of the world—will be acknowledged and accepted as the One who speaks to humankind as God's Prophet, High Priest and King. I have endeavoured to write so as to 'let the Word do its work'.

In the seventh century AD a man known today as the prophet Muhammad founded another religion that is now called 'Islam'.[3] Today, it boasts over 1.6 billion adherents, and some expect it to be the largest religion by 2070. Its origins are found in the Arab culture. Its teachings represent a mixture of Old Testament (OT) and New Testament (NT) content and some non-Bible sources in Zoroastrianism, producing a new and different worldview from the Judaeo-Christian ethos. We will not engage with the disputes between the sects of Islam but accept that 'Allah is not the deity of a Sunni or Shiah or Wahhabi sect, but the object of devotion of them all'.[4]

This book is not about the history of Islam and its founder Muhammad, who no doubt was sincere in his search for the one true God; nor is it an analysis of Islamic political attitudes and social structures. Rather, it is an examination of Islam's doctrinal views based on a comparison of the texts of the Bible and the Quran. Islam claims to be a religion sent from God (Allah), but what does the Bible say? There is much speculation about the origin of the Quran in literature; however, it is not necessary to my examination of Islam as to whether or not Muhammad received the Quran as a whole book, perfect and true, from the archangel Gabriel (Jibril). I am concerned with what the Quran and Islam teach and the claims they make for Muhammad, the founder of Islam; thus I keep my comments on those matters to a minimum while discussing what Christians believe. In order to present the widest scope of Islamic belief and to show that Islam in all its forms makes the same attack on biblical Christianity, I have quoted Islamic sources fairly with the understanding that variations apply in some Muslim sects. Help in writing this book has been found from various resources. Where direct quotations are used they have been acknowledged. Where general issues and details regarding Islamic practices are discussed, please see the Select Bibliography for my sources.

The history of Islam is well documented and its teachings are well known, especially its five duties called the 'Five Pillars of Islam'. Christians may ask, however, whether this is enough to validate Islam's claim to be an alternative to and a substitute for Bible Christianity. Does adhering to its 'Five Pillars' either fully or in part make one fit for heaven? Is Muhammad's claim to be God's final prophet acceptable to Christians?

Foreword

This book examines these assertions. If Islam is free to deny and challenge the Christian Scripture's view of its Messiah Jesus Christ and its worldview without political reproach and interference, I reserve the right to challenge Islam's religious views and put forward the counter religious arguments for Bible integrity, authority and sufficiency, upholding the view that Jesus Christ is God's last Prophet to the world before the Second Coming and Judgement Day.

Thanks must go to those who have helped me produce this work by giving advice on Islamic doctrine and suggested reading. Several have made helpful contributions to the text: my friends, John Dickson, Pastor Juge Ram and Paul Barnes, and not forgetting my son. I also thank both Pastor Edward Challen and Nadia, whose knowledge of Islam has been a considerable and invaluable help for which I am grateful first to our Saviour in heaven and also to them both. I also thank my publishers for their help and support in getting this book into print and into the hands of God's people everywhere. However, I take all responsibility for its content.

Rev. Ian S. McNaughton

NOTES

1 'The split into Sunni and Shia originated little more than 20 years after Muhammad's death in a dispute over the succession to leadership of the Muslim community.' Patrick Sookhdeo, *A Pocket Guide to Islam* (Fearn, Ross-shire: Christian Focus, 2010), p. 103.

2 *Luther's Works*, vol. 51, Sermons I, ed. J. J. Pelikan, H. C. Oswald and H. T. Lehmann (Philadelphia: Fortress, 1959), pp. 77–78.

3 Islam means 'submission' (Sura 3:19).

4 Introduction, S. M. Zwemer, *The Moslem Doctrine of God* (American Tract Society; repr. Gerrards Cross: WEC Press, 1981), p. 6.

The use of the term 'Scripture' is widely used among Muslims to stand for the Quran, while for Christianity it speaks of the Bible, the sixty-six books that make up the Old and New Testaments.[1] The Quran is the holy book of Islam and is believed by Muslims to have been written by one man, Muhammad.

The Bible is made up of twenty-seven New Testament books and thirty-nine Old Testament books (the latter were the Hebrew Scriptures Jesus Christ used).[2] They were written over a period of around 1,500 years and by around forty authors. Although written by so many at such different times there is, nevertheless, an extraordinary agreement on the knowledge of God and His covenant promises. The Old Testament Scriptures were translated into Greek for the Jewish Diaspora before Jesus was born and this version, the Septuagint (LXX), became the Old Testament Bible for the Gentile churches. To this the twenty-seven books of the New Testament were added, completing the sixty-six-book canon. The Christian church accepted the Jewish Tanakh (the Law, Prophets and Writings) which consists of the same books as the Christian Old Testament canon, although in a slightly different order and with other minor differences. The Tanakh contains thirty-nine books in all (if each of the Twelve Minor Prophets is counted as one and the subdivided books such as Kings and Chronicles are counted as two). The five books of the Torah, twenty-one books of the Prophets and thirteen books of Writings make up the thirty-nine. Most books were written in Hebrew except for Ezra, Daniel and one verse in Jeremiah, which are in Aramaic.

The Islamic canon is today made up of three sources: the Quran, the Hadith and the Sunna.[3] Sunna means 'the way of the prophet'. 'The *sunnah* [as the Hadith] is essential to entering into heavenly portals. [It was] relevant because the final redaction and collation of the Quran had not occurred, so the guide for ethics was the life of Muhammad itself. One must obey the *sunnah* just as the Quran in order to gain entry to Paradise.'[4] The Quran is believed to have been revealed to Muhammad section by section over twenty-three years (AD 610–632) while the Hadith, a collection of sayings which speak of both public and private religious practices, were handed down over a longer period. After Muhammad's death, 'many salutary sayings which were thought to be in accord with his sentiments were added'. This corpus was vastly expanded 'during subsequent generations'.[5] All that was required for a saying to receive respectability was for it to be attributed to an *isnad* (see below). This, if true, means that many of the sayings reckoned to Muhammad were not his![6] Contrast this with the sayings of Jesus recorded in the Gospels, which are clear and unaltered for all to read. These were attributed to his three years of earthly ministry, but the visions of Muhammad were received over twenty-three years and his supposed sayings (hadiths) were added to by his followers after his death.

The Quran has 114 suras (chapters)[7] and is about two-thirds the size of the New Testament. For someone unfamiliar with Islam it can be confusing to cross-reference different versions of the Quran as there are different systems of numbering the verses, and the total number of verses ranges from 6,204 to 6,360, depending on the translation.[8] 'To Muslims, the Qur'an is the word of God "vowel for vowel, syllable for syllable".'[9] It is alleged to have been revealed in Arabic to Muhammad through the angel Gabriel. 'The traditional belief is that there was no human contribution to the process. God's word was conveyed verbatim to Muhammad.'[10] The chapters are arranged according to length but have no subject continuity, nor are they listed in the order that they were received.[11] Islam claims that the Quranic text is the purest there is in all literature: 'There is probably in the world no other book which has remained twelve centuries [now fourteen] with so pure a text.'[12] 'Because the original Arabic text is ambiguous and hard to understand, any translations that seem clear and comprehensible have certainly had a considerable amount of editorial input. Modern translations are being used to promote radical Islam around the world.'[13]

The Hadith and Sunna of Muhammad

The Sunna constitutes the authenticated traditions believed to be the words of Muhammad memorized by his followers and written down. This massive corpus is 'compiled from thousands of individual brief narratives each of which is referred to individually also as a *hadith*, with a small "h".'[14] The origin of any hadith statement is said to have been attested by companions of Muhammad. These were guarantors intended to support the authenticity and accuracy of each hadith document and who are known as the *isnad*. The established Sunna is as reliable as the Quran and they are the only primary sources for understanding Islam. Sunna together with the Quran is the basis for political, legal and doctrinal Islam.

What does Islam think of the Bible?

'Muslims believe that the original messages transmitted by previous prophets, including Moses and Jesus, were essentially the same as the message brought by Muhammad and preserved in the Quran.'[15] When the message differs, they say it is the Bible that is in error. There is no evidence that this is the case and no proof to support this dogma. Because of this teaching the integrity of the Christian Scriptures is questioned and the Word of God is regarded as untrustworthy. This 'Theory of Corruption' is taught to children of school age in mosques and madrasas.[16]

Translation of the Quran

It is necessary to say something about the use of Quranic translations. Islam holds that every translation of the Quran from Arabic is only that, a translation, and it does not hold the same authority as the Arabic version. This gives me a problem when writing in English and quoting from English translations of the Quran. I have therefore used one English translation, namely, Maulana Wahiduddin Khan, *The Quran: A New Translation*, ed. Farida Khanam (New Delhi: Goodword Books, 2009).

All other quotes from the Quran are reproduced as they were found in the sources I used.

The way of salvation

Muslims claim to teach the Ten Commandments (of Jews and Christians) to children at an early age and that the Quran is compatible with them.[17] The reality, however, is that there is no power to obey them because of original sin and thus the righteousness of holiness which the Ten Commandments demand is wanting in practice. God looks on the heart, and when He sees faith in Jesus Christ He imputes to the believer the righteousness of Christ who took sin to Himself (2 Cor. 5:21).

Jesus fulfilled God's law by His life and through His death, but Islam, having rejected both Judaism and Christianity, made a new law of religion under the guise of the 'Five Pillars of Islam' (see Chapter 14). Thus Islam rejects the holy and atoning work of Jesus Christ and ignores its religious implications for lost sinners. This has resulted in Islam ignoring the Old Testament prophecies, the doctrine of original sin and God's revealed way of salvation through Jesus Christ alone (John 14:6). Islam has invented another road to heaven which, to paraphrase Paul, is 'another gospel' (Gal. 1:6–8). This rejection is a return to religious legalism and is a folly which is decreed to fail. Legalism, the view that salvation depends on strict adherence to the laws and precepts of God, is seen in the use of the 'Five Pillars' to gain Allah's favour as a way of salvation. The choice since Muhammad's day is between Islamic legalism and God's free grace in Christ Jesus.

Jesus Christ our risen Saviour is able to forgive sins. Here is good news: our guilty consciences can be silenced; all our sins can be forgiven; our hearts can feel the touch of His cleansing blood. The paralytic man in Capernaum was forgiven by Jesus: 'Man, your sins are forgiven you' (Luke 5:20). A man's sin is his greatest problem, and spiritual health is of far greater importance than physical wholeness. When Jesus saw the faith of that paralytic man, the first thing He did was to forgive him all his sins. It was only after this that He dealt with his physical needs. Let none think he has no sins to confess or transgressions to be forgiven. Faith, not works (however great or submissive), is the door to forgiveness and justification. Those who come to the throne of grace in faith will receive acceptance, access to God and assurance of salvation, all because of Jesus Christ's atoning death.

Jesus' miracles and ministry are rejected by Islam if they do not appear to fit with the Muslim worldview. However, the Bible itself says that no new teaching (revelation) is required following the ascension of Jesus Christ forty days after His resurrection. The ascended Jesus now sits in session reigning over God's kingdom until the Second Coming (1 Cor. 15:24–25). To embrace another religious text as superior to the sixty-six books is unacceptable to Christians and is against the express teaching of Jesus Christ and the inspired New Testament writers (Luke 16:17; John 10:35; Acts 4:12; 2 Tim. 3:15–16; Heb. 1:1–2; 2 Peter 1:19–21; 3:2, 16; 1 John 2:22).

Islam treats Jesus Christ as a holy and good man and the Messiah of Israel, but it does not encourage its followers to read His words or to read the prophets and writers of the Old and New Testaments who reveal His glory. In fact, countries like Saudi Arabia ban the Scriptures. For instance, Umar, one of Muhammad's companions, read a copy of the Torah translated into Arabic (the Jews used to translate the Torah into Arabic). Abu Hurayrah said, 'The people of the Scripture [Jews] used to recite the Torah in Hebrew and explain it in Arabic to the Muslims. On that, the Messenger of Allaah said, "Do not believe the people of the Scripture or disbelieve them, but say: {We believe in Allaah and what is revealed to us}"' (Sura 2:136, Al-Bukhari). This was explicitly stated in another version of this hadith narrated by Al-Bazzaar on the authority of Jaabir. He said,

Umar copied part of the Torah in Arabic, brought it to the Prophet, and began to read it to him. As he read, the Prophet's face changed colour. One of the men of the Ansaar said, 'Woe to you Ibn Al-Khattaab! Can you not see the face of the Messenger of Allaah?' Thereupon, the Prophet said, 'Do not ask the People of the Book about anything for they will not guide you when they have gone astray. (If you listen to them) You will either disbelieve in what is right or believe in what is false. By Allaah, if Moses had been alive today, he would have been obliged to follow me.'

This rejection of the Bible (OT and NT) is because Muslims are taught:
- That the Christian texts of Scripture are corrupted;
- That salvation comes to us by way of the 'Five Pillars of Islam' and not through the atoning blood of Jesus Christ;
- That Jesus was only a man born of the virgin Mary and not the Son of God incarnate;
- That there is no greater prophet than their own prophet Muhammad;
- That the Quran alone is the word of God.

I have deliberately set out to preach Christ and through Him God's way of salvation by free and unmerited grace, for 'Salvation is of the LORD' (Jonah 2:9).

NOTES

1 When the terms 'Bible' or 'Word of God' are mentioned in this work they refer to the Christian Scriptures.

2 The Roman Catholic and Orthodox Churches add another fifteen deuterocanonical books which they believe to have equal standing with the other sixty-six. Protestantism, however, sees these books only as non-inspired historical Jewish writings written in the four hundred years between the end of the Old and the beginning of the New Testaments. They lack the marks of divine inspiration.

3 I am grateful here for the help of John Burton, *An Introduction to the Hadith* (Edinburgh: Edinburgh University Press, 1994).

4 Patrick Sookhdeo, *Understanding Islamic Theology* (MacLean, VA: Isaac Publishing, 2103), pp. 372–373.

5 Ignaz Goldziher, *Muhammedanische Studie*n, quoted in Burton, *Introduction to the Hadith*, pp. ix, x.

6 Muslims are aware of this as the hadiths are classified as *Sahih* (authentic), *Hasan* (strong narration but not as strong as *Sahih*) or *Dhaaif* (weak), depending on the strength of the narration chain. Most Muslims would adhere to the *Sahih* hadiths (e.g. in the Bukhari, Muslim and other collections). They will argue that the weak hadiths are on less important matters and are not necessary to the basics of faith.

7 'It is not easy to determine whether Sura means a whole chapter, or part only of a chapter, or is used in the sense of "revelation".' The Quran (Rodwell edn, 1876), Sura 96, 'Thick Blood, or Clots of Blood', footnote 1, at https://www.sacred-texts.com/isl/qr/096.htm. In this book I have used it as meaning 'chapter'.

8 Steven Masood, *The Bible and the Qur'an: A Question of Integrity* (Carlisle: Paternoster / Authentic Lifestyle, 2001), pp. 3–4.

9 Ibid., p. 4.

10 Ibid., p. 5.

11 For a chronological listing, see https://archive.org/details/TheKoranTranslatedByRodwell.

12 Ahmed Deedat, *Is the Bible God's Word?* (Durban: Islamic Propagation Centre International, 1989), p. 8.

13 Patrick Sookhdeo, *A Pocket Guide to Islam* (Fern, Ross-shire: Christian Focus / Isaac Publishing, 2010), p. 42.

14 Burton, *Introduction to the Hadith*, p. ix.

15 Masood, *The Bible and the Qur'an*, p. xv.

16 Ibid., p. xvi.

17 'These commandments are among the core teachings of Judaism and Christianity that are taught to children at an early age, and all of them are included within the teachings of Islam.' 'The Ten Commandments in Islam', Faith in Allah, https://abuaminaelias.com/the-ten-commandments-in-islam/.

The doctrine of God

Can you search out the deep things of God?

Can you find out the limits of the Almighty? (Job 11:7)

Muslims say, 'God is great', and while Christians have no hesitation in affirming this greatness, we need to clarify the more basic issue of what we mean when we talk about 'God'.[1] What makes God what He is? To this question Christians answer, 'God is a spirit, infinite, eternal and unchangeable, in His being, wisdom, power, holiness, justice, goodness and truth.'[2] This question is to be distinguished from the more usual question asked about God, namely, 'Who is God?' 'What is God?' asks about His nature and being, while 'Who is God?' asks about His relationship to His creatures and creation. We cannot answer the 'What is God?' question adequately as the finite cannot comprehend the Infinite. However, God has revealed Himself through His attributes, in creation and through His self-revelation in His written Word, the Bible. They tell us what and who God is and they reveal those essential qualities which are the Being of God. Both Martin Luther and John Calvin said that we can know God in His hiddenness but that His essence remains shrouded in impenetrable darkness. His attributes are natural to and innate in Himself. God is a self-conscious and a self-determining Being. He has no parts and no body. When the Bible speaks of the 'hands' or 'body' of God it speaks anthropomorphically or figuratively because He far transcends our human knowledge. The Being of God does not admit of any scientific definition yet we are not ignorant of God's character for we have the Bible. From the scriptural record we have the answer to the question 'Who is God?' as it is revealed to us in the relationship He had with Israel, His chosen people:

Chapter 1

'You are My witnesses,' says the LORD,
'And My servant whom I have chosen,
That you may know and believe Me,
And understand that I am He.
Before Me there was no God formed,
Nor shall there be after Me.' (Isa. 43:1)

The Scriptures reveal the true nature of God. Through His involvement with Israel and the surrounding nations we have a record of what He thinks, what He likes and dislikes, what He is in His eternal nature and what He demands from His people and the nations of the world. This is not historiography but revelation.[3]

Can we know more about God than what is revealed in the Bible? The canon is closed, and every generation of Christians in every cultural context must seek to see how God is speaking to them in and through Scripture. It is essential that we seek peace with God and learn experimentally that He is our Father in heaven (Matt. 6:9).

The Trinity

Islam believes that 'God is a solitary monad with unity only'.[4] He is alone and therefore cannot be known. However, the Bible teaches God to be 'Three in One' and 'One in Three'. There is no god other than God the Almighty—one God in three Persons, Father, Son and Holy Spirit, co-equal and co-eternal, without division or confusion of natures. Although the term 'Trinity' is not present in the Christian Scriptures, the concept and doctrine is. The divine 'Three in One' stretches through all the ages which are gone and those which are yet to come.

'The Islamic doctrine of God is centred on power and will. There is virtually no room for love.'[5] However, the Christian Scriptures teach that as Creator, God, by supernatural power, created man on day 6 of creation week:

Then God said, 'Let Us make man in Our image, according to Our likeness; let them have dominion over the fish of the sea, over the birds of the air, and over the cattle, over all the earth and over every creeping thing that creeps on the earth.' So God created man in His own image; in the image of God He created him; male and female He created them. (Gen. 1:26–27)

Being created 'in *Our* image' is a Trinitarian statement. Hebrew has both singular and plural verb forms like other languages but it also has a *dual* form which is used when two (pairs) are spoken of. Thus this phrase 'in *Our* image', being in the plural form, speaks of more than two. 'The Christian doctrine of personhood flows from the Christian doctrine of the three persons who are God.'[6] An important (root) name for God in the Hebrew Old Testament is *El*, of which *Elohim* is the plural form, even though it is usually translated in the singular. Some scholars hold that the plural form refers to the triune God of Genesis 1:26, who made man in His own image. *Elohim* conveys the idea that the one Supreme Being, who is the only true God, in some sense exists in a plural form.[7]

An early Christian creed makes it plain that the New Testament church taught and accepted the doctrine of the Trinity: 'We believe in one God, the Father . . . and in one Lord Jesus Christ . . . and in one Holy Spirit, the Lord and Life-giver, that proceeds from the Father' (The Nicene Creed, 'found in Epiphanius, *Ancoratus* 118, *c.* AD 374, and extracted by scholars, almost word for word, from the Catechetical Lectures of S. Cyril of Jerusalem').[8]

Is God knowable?

The Bible does not prove the existence of God, but assumes that He exists and declares Him to be omniscient (all-knowing, John 21:17b), omnipotent (all-powerful, Matt. 19:26) and omnipresent (everywhere present, Ps. 139:7–12). Because of His transcendence the early Church Fathers felt that it was impossible to gain an adequate knowledge of the divine essence. The Protestant Reformers agreed that the essence of God is incomprehensible but they did not exclude all knowledge of it. They stated the unity, simplicity and spirituality of God. So God in His Being is incomprehensible (Job 11:7), immaterial (John 4:24) and unchangeable (Exod. 3:14–15). God communicates the knowledge of Himself to man and can be known only as He actively makes Himself known. He is the *subject* of such knowledge—He communicates it; and He is the *object* of that knowledge—He is known through the knowledge conveyed to us in revelation. Therefore, if there is no revelation, there is no knowledge of God. Revelation is God *actively* making Himself known. This is a supernatural act of self-communication mediated through creation and the Holy Bible. However, not all people understand this because 'the natural man does not receive the things of the Spirit of God, for they are foolishness to him; nor can he know them, because they are spiritually discerned' (1 Cor. 2:14).

There is an acquired knowledge of God and there is also an innate knowledge peculiar to humans as creatures made in the image of God (Gen. 1:26; Rom. 1:19). Theologians prefer to talk of 'engrafted or implanted' knowledge, but evolutionists deny both. The innate knowledge is ours by birth while acquired knowledge is gained by the study of God's revelation both in nature and in the Bible (Rom. 1:19–23). The Reformers said that even natural revelation has been obscured by the fall, thus men cannot read it aright. Therefore, God in the Bible 'republished the truths of natural revelation to clear them of misrepresentation and to interpret them for us'. Not only this, but God 'provided a cure for spiritual blindness in the work of regeneration and sanctification so that we can obtain a true knowledge of God'. It is foolish to ignore this revelation of God in the Bible, and to substitute another image or other images of Him is tantamount to idolatry! Louis Berkhof says, 'All our knowledge of God is derived from his self-revelation in nature and in Scripture. Consequently our knowledge of God is true and accurate, since it is a copy of the archetypal knowledge which God has of Himself.'[9]

When God made Himself known to Abraham He said that He was *El Shaddai*, that is, the only God, the mighty God, the Ruler and King of all creation (Gen. 17:1ff.). Age to age He is still the same and the God who is love:

El Shaddai [God Almighty], El Shaddai,

El-Elyon[10] na Adonai [God in the highest, O Lord]

Age to age you're still the same

By the power of the name.

El Shaddai, El Shaddai,

Erkamka na Adonai [We will love You, O Lord]

We will praise and lift you high,

El Shaddai.[11]

MOSES

God the covenant Father of Israel made Himself known to Moses, speaking to him at the burning bush: 'He said, "I am the God of your father—the God of Abraham, the God of Isaac, and the God of Jacob." And Moses hid his face, for he was afraid to look upon God' (Exod. 3:6). God reassured Moses that He was the God of his forefathers—Abraham, Isaac and Jacob. This was a fuller revelation of the One whom they had known and a reassuring word of hope and truth. The Angel of the LORD spoke as if he was God (v. 4). Moses now stood on holy ground (v. 5). The four-consonant Hebrew word used in Exodus 3:4, YHWH (the Tetragrammaton), translated for us as 'LORD', reveals the true speaker, namely, God Himself (v. 4). It is one word, 'Yahweh', with the vowels of another (*Adonai*). Some English translations of the Bible vocalize the word as Jehovah, while others use Yahweh. At the burning bush Moses saw the LORD who burns like a fire yet remains the same and never diminishes. The author of the Epistle to the Hebrews is conscious of this attribute at 12:18, 29 (cf. Exod. 24:17). The word YHWH is so sacred to Jews that they do not pronounce it. They refuse to say the written name but rather use *Adonai* when in prayer or reading the Torah, a practice still used today in the synagogue.

Moses heard God saying to him, 'I AM WHO I AM' (Exod. 3:14), a declaration that 'all the majesty, all the supremacy, all the glory of absolute and essential Deity, are His inherent right'.[12] God revealed to Moses His eternal self-existence and His unchanging character; He is the same yesterday, today and for ever.

When time shall have expired, He still is, 'I AM THAT I AM'. If there had been the moment when His being dawned, His name would be, 'I am what I was not'. If there could be a moment when his being must have end, His name would be, 'I am what I shall not be'. But He is 'I AM THAT I AM'.[13]

The immensity of God's divine essence was laid before Moses in that encounter. 'God is ever being and ever acting.'[14] 'I AM WHO I AM' reveals that He is self-existent, self-contained and absolutely independent, while the New Testament reveals that 'God is Spirit' and 'God is love' (John 4:24; 1 John 4:8).

THE FATHERHOOD OF GOD

God's self-revelation to David was one of the most extraordinary of all in the Old Testament's thirty-nine books. It is seen in the Psalms of David where God is embraced as David's Shepherd and also intimately as his Father. In the famous Psalm 23 David is assured that God is looking after him personally: 'The LORD is my shepherd; I shall not want' (v. 1). This conviction covers the whole experience of life, from physical well-being, to spiritual renewal and protection, to daily peace, and it includes the strong belief that 'Surely goodness and mercy shall follow me all the days of my life; and I will dwell in the house of the LORD forever' (v. 6). Personal and individual sonship is also a blessing to David, who considers God to be a 'father of the fatherless' (Ps. 68:5) and his own Father: 'You are my Father, My God, and the rock of my salvation' (Ps. 89:26). Psalm 89 contains a long poetic description of the covenant which God had made with David (see 2 Sam. 7). God was more to David than a distant deity or an enduring belief; He was One full of loving faithfulness personally known and experienced.[15] Thus to David, God was a loving Father: 'As a father pities his children, so the LORD pities those who fear Him' (Ps. 103:13).

ISRAEL

God likens Himself to a father in relation to the people of Israel in the book of the prophet Malachi (1:6):

A son honors his father,
And a servant his master.
If then I am the Father,
Where is My honor?
And if I am a Master,
Where is My reverence?
Says the LORD of hosts.

The Father of Israel is to be honoured and obeyed, says the prophet, and His name is to be reverenced. Another, greater than Malachi, agreed: 'Our Father in heaven, hallowed be Your name' (Luke 11:2).[16] It was the Father who provided the lamb of sacrifice to save Isaac's life (Gen. 22:7–8, 13). From these accounts we see that God is great in His almightiness and God is love in His Fatherhood.

The Holy Spirit

The Holy Spirit is mentioned three times in the Quran (Suras 16:104; 2:81 and 254). The last mention is a statement that Jesus was helped by the Holy Spirit. However, this truth is invalidated because 'all the Muslim commentators are agreed that the Holy Spirit in this passage means the angel Gabriel'![17]

There is no awareness in Islam of the need for the presence of the Holy Spirit to know and worship God aright, for Islam has no concept of the Holy Spirit's ministry. There is no desire for His help and no consciousness of His relevance to true worship (John 4:24). Ultimately, this is due to the lack of personal salvation in Islam—a concept Islam does not recognize but one that is clearly evident in the New Testament. For instance, Muslims have no concept of the new birth (John 3:5; 1 John 5:1), the 'ministry of the Spirit' (2 Cor. 3:8, 17), nor the 'sealing of the Spirit' (2 Cor. 1:22; Eph. 1:13–14; 4:30). Thus a personal relationship with God is denied them.

The New Testament

The classic understanding of the Trinity is grasped in those scriptural texts and passages where the three Persons are spoken of together in holy harmony and in works of power and grace. The following examples reveal the doctrinal foundation for the Trinity:

And Jesus came and spoke to them, saying, 'All authority has been given to Me in heaven and on earth. Go therefore and make disciples of all the nations, baptizing them in the name of the Father and of the Son and of the Holy Spirit.' (Matt. 28:18–19)

But when the Helper comes, whom I [Jesus] shall send to you from the Father, the Spirit of truth who proceeds from the Father, He will testify of Me. (John 15:26)

The grace of the Lord Jesus Christ, and the love of God, and the communion of the Holy Spirit be with you all. Amen. (2 Cor. 13:14)

NOTES

1 I am indebted to Louis Berkhof, *Systematic Theology* (London: Banner of Truth Trust, 1971) for much of what follows.

2 Westminster Shorter Catechism, Q. 4.

3 Historiography is an attempt to relay the *significance* of history whether true or not: 'the art of writing history'.

4 Robert Letham, *The Holy Trinity* (Phillipsburg, NJ: Presbyterian & Reformed, 2004), p. 442.

5 Ibid.

6 Peter Toon, 'Our Triune God', quoted in Letham, *Holy Trinity*, p. 442.

7 The plural idea of *Elohim* is distinctly conveyed in Gen. 1:26; see *The Hebrew Student Manual* (London: Samuel Bagster & Sons, [n. d.]), Genesis, p. 1.

8 Henry Bettenson, 'The Nicene Creed', *Documents of the Christian Church* (London: Oxford University Press, 1974), pp. 25–26.

9 Berkhof, *Systematic Theology*, p. 35. I am indebted to Berkhof for his help here.

10 EL ELYON (*God Most High*): a Hebrew name for God. Translated into English, it means God Most High (Gen. 14:18).

11 Michael Card, *Mission Praise*, no. 119 (1990).

12 Henry Law, *The Gospel in Exodus* (London: Banner of Truth Trust, 1967), p. 13.

13 Ibid., p. 14.

14 John D. Currid, *Exodus*, Vol. 1 (Darlington: Evangelical Press, 2000), p. 396, n. 24.

15 Verses 19–37 of this psalm have an eternal messianic fulfilment in Jesus Christ who is the 'Root and the Offspring of David' (Rom. 1:2–4; Rev. 22:16).

16 In the New Testament, 'God' (Gk *Theos*) is equivalent to *El, Elohim, Elyon*, while 'Lord' (Gk *kurios*) is equivalent to 'Jehovah'/'Yahweh'.

17 S. M. Zwemer, *The Moslem Doctrine of God* (American Tract Society; repr. Gerrards Cross: WEC Press, 1981), p. 88. In the Muhsen Khan Translation (suras 16:102; 253) but the third reference is missing.

Worshipping God the Almighty

You shall worship no other god, for the LORD, whose name is Jealous, is a jealous God. (Exod. 34:14)

I slam's concept of worship is very different from that of Christianity. Perhaps the only similarity is the professed fear of God. There is, for instance, no inclusive worship in Islam because there is no equality of the sexes. Some Christian groups still separate male and female worshippers, usually placing them on either side of the church aisle, but they still participate together in public worship. An example of this is the Amish community in the USA. Muslim women, however, although allowed to go to the mosque for prayers on Friday, are physically isolated from male worshippers. They are not together and they are not seen together. This is because there is no sense of male–female moral or spiritual equality in Islam. Consider the following passages:

The wives have rights corresponding to those which the husbands have, according to what is recognised to be fair, but men have a rank above them. (Sura 2:228)

Once Allah's Apostle went out to the Musalla (to offer the prayer) 'Id-al-Adha or Al-Fitr prayer. Then he passed by the women and said, 'O women! Give alms, as I have seen that the majority of the dwellers of Hell-fire were you (women).' They asked, 'Why is it so, O Allah's Apostle?' He replied, 'You curse frequently and are ungrateful to your husbands. *I have not seen anyone more deficient in intelligence and religion than you. A cautious sensible man could be led astray by some of you.*' The women asked, 'O Allah's Apostle! What is deficient in our intelligence and religion?' He said, *'Is not the evidence of two women equal to the witness of one man?'* They replied in the affirmative. He said, *'This is the deficiency in her intelligence.* Isn't it true that a woman can neither pray nor fast during her menses?' The women replied in the affirmative. He said, 'This is the deficiency in her religion.'[1]

This separation is contrary to New Testament rules on worship which state that there is neither male nor female in Christ (Gal. 3:28), and it ignores Jesus Christ's teaching on worship which tells us that the Holy Spirit is needed to worship God properly (John 4:21–24).

Prayer[2]

Prayer is one of the 'Five Pillars of Islam', and for the Muslim it is 'a means of bringing mankind closer to Allah'. Muslims must start and end each day with prayer. Daily prayer (Salāt) is an 'essential obligatory duty' in Islam which must be performed five times a day at fixed hours. Prayers are regarded as very important for salvation, and 'the performance of Friday Prayer entails a great deal of virtues and forgiveness from Allah'.[3] This highlights Islam as a religion of works and not grace; of human effort and not love. Prayer is defined as worship and is to be performed as instructed, remembering that one is standing before one's Creator. In prayer, one must stand facing the direction of the Ka'bah, bow and kneel. One must then recite the opening chapter of the Quran praising and glorifying Allah, and asking for his support and help. Sura Alfateeh 1:6, 7 is an example: 'Guide us to the Straight Way. The Way of those on whom You have bestowed Your Grace, not (the way) of those who earned Your Anger (such as the Jews), nor of those who went astray (such as the Christians).'[4] This prayer, as prescribed, is to be learned by all Muslims. All Islamic sects and groups say this prayer. No Muslim prayer is valid without it.

The approved (stinted)[5] prayers of Islam are a very powerful tool in the religion's armoury. They consist of set texts that bind the conscience of the worshipper and at the same time condemn rival religions, making them appear inferior.[6] The Muslim who prays five times a day will repeat this prayer at least seventeen times.

FRIDAY PRAYERS

Muslims believe that the divinely ordered day of prayer (worship) is Friday. 'There are many hadith [traditions] of the Prophet indicating the importance, excellency and superiority of Friday.'[7] The Hadith says, 'The best day on which the sun rises is Friday. On that day was Adam born . . . and on that day he was entered into paradise. And on that day he was expelled from Paradise. And the hour will only be established on Friday.'[8]

Friday is regarded as among the 'numerous bounties that Allah has blessed the Ummah[9] of Islam with'. Since humans were created to worship God, and Adam was created on a Friday, it is fitting, according to Islam, that Muslims spend that day in worship. However, according to Muhammad Asad, while Friday prayer at noon is obligatory, Friday is not a day of compulsory rest in Islamic law. Friday prayers were initiated as Muhammad's way to spite the Jews and the Christians since, for Christians, Sunday was the special day of worship, and for Jews it was the Saturday Sabbath. In other words, while for Jews and Christians the reason for honouring Saturday and Sunday had religious roots, for Muhammad Friday prayer was a political statement. Muhammad himself said,

O you who have attained to faith! When the call to prayer is sounded on the day of congregation, hasten to the remembrance of God, and leave all worldly commerce: this is for your own good, if you but knew it. And when the prayer is ended, disperse freely on earth and seek to obtain (something) of God's bounty; but remember God often, so that you might attain to a happy state! Yet (it does happen that) when people become aware of (an occasion for) worldly gain or a passing delight, they rush head-long towards it, and leave thee standing (and preaching). Say: 'That which is with God is far better than all passing delight and all gain! And God is the best of providers!' (Sura 62:9–11)[10]

ABLUTIONS

Before the compulsory (for men) congregational prayer on Friday, ablutions (*Wudu'*) are to be performed, because 'Allah does not accept prayers without Ablution'.[11] These ablutions include washing the hands, rinsing the mouth and nose, washing the face and forearms, and washing the ears and feet up to the ankles. Prayer is thus regarded as a deed of righteousness deserving of reward (Al-Baqarab, 2:277).[12] The Christian's 'ablutions', however, are to be found in Jesus Christ. On repentance of personal sin we are washed in Christ's atoning blood, while the personal prayers of believing Christians (alone or with others) are not so much a duty or a chore as moments of communion with their Father in heaven through the merits of the Son, Jesus Christ, aided by the Holy Spirit.[13]

Why do Christians not worship on a Friday?

Christians worship on the first day of the week—Sunday—because their Saviour rose from the dead on that day after three days in the tomb. This recognizes the significance of that resurrection event. Gathering Sunday by Sunday is a powerful and public testimony that 'He is risen indeed'. Christianity is based on fact, not fiction.

The first day of the week signifying the day when Jesus rose from the dead is the *sign* proclaiming Jesus' glory and messianic mission. The resurrection was the ultimate sign for the apostles. Jesus spoke of His resurrection to the disciples before His death, but He revealed it slowly and only from time to time (see Matt. 16:21ff.). Peter's confession of Jesus' messianic role was a turning point in the understanding of that disciple as to who Jesus was: Jesus 'said to them, "But who do you say that I am?" Simon Peter answered and said, "You are the Christ, the Son of the living God." Jesus answered and said to him, "Blessed are you, Simon Bar-Jonah, for flesh and blood has not revealed this to you, but My Father who is in heaven"' (Matt. 16:15–17). The Father had given light and truth to the apostles. And from that point on, Jesus spoke of His death and resurrection more often (Matt. 17:9, 22–23; 20:17–19).

We cannot physically see the risen Jesus in His resurrected and glorified body, for He is in heaven; nor were we at the empty tomb that first resurrection morning; but the contemporary eyewitnesses were, and they have recorded it for us in the New Testament. Herman Ridderbos puts this well: 'The Gospel is not the story of the later faith of the Christian church; it is the report of the revelation of God in the flesh. But only the end, the resurrection and the Spirit teach disciples to understand the beginning and to offer faith a foothold "in the word that Jesus had spoken".'[14]

The weekly Christian day of rest, every first day of the week, points fifty-two times a year to Jesus Christ's triumph over death and Satan. This is a powerful witness to the mission and gospel of Jesus Christ. Without a weekly Christian Lord's Day the resurrection would be so marginalized it would hardly be noticed after two thousand years. God has seen to it that it is still remembered, and not only by the church but also by the world, through the weekly event we call the Lord's Day (Rev. 1:10). If Christian believers stop gathering together to worship on this ordained day of the first day of the week, this powerful testimony of the Christian Lord's Day-Sabbath will be silenced. If there is no Sabbath day rest, the sign of the resurrection will be lost to the world.

The weekly Christian Sabbath is therefore God's sign to the world about the resurrection of Jesus Christ from the dead. Islam disregards the importance of the Lord's Day-Sabbath sign because it denies the historic third-day resurrection of Christ Jesus.

Access to God

According to the Islamic Albirr Foundation UK, prayer is 'the most important pillar of Islam' and act of atonement since through the use of the five daily prayers 'Allah washes away the sins'.[15] The same erroneous belief that prayer can atone for personal sins can be found in the Old Testament at the time of Israel's exodus from Egypt, when prayer alone was insufficient to propitiate God Almighty for the sins of Israel. God in His grace supplied for each Israelite family a Passover lamb whose shed blood was required to make atonement for every house (Exod. 12). However, no lamb was given to the Egyptians. Imagine, for a moment, an Egyptian parent on the night of the tenth plague, kneeling in prayer and in the fear of God Almighty and praying, 'Lord God, please do not kill my son—my only son, whom I love.' Was he heard? No. Why? He was *not* heard because there was no atoning blood, and no faith in its power to redeem. Thus, if worship is to be accepted by God, there is need for a Saviour whose blood remits sin. Jesus Christ is the antitype of the Passover lamb. He died to save all who put their trust in His atoning blood, whatever their background or nationality:

the blood of Christ, who through the eternal Spirit offered Himself without spot to God, [will] cleanse your conscience from dead works . . . For Christ has not entered the holy places made with hands, which are copies of the true, but into heaven itself, now to appear in the presence of God for us . . . He has appeared to put away sin by the sacrifice of Himself. (Heb. 9:14, 24, 26b)

Christian worship is the blood-bought soul coming to God to offer up spiritual sacrifices. From the Epistle of First Peter we learn that true worship starts after conversion: 'Since you have purified your souls in obeying the truth through the Spirit . . . having been born again . . . offer up spiritual sacrifices acceptable to God through Jesus Christ' (1 Peter 1:22–23; 2:5). Thus true worship of God flows to God via the regenerating work of the Holy Spirit and through Jesus Christ the only Mediator between God and men. True worshippers are described in 1 Peter 2:5 as 'living stones' and as a 'holy priesthood'. They are called such because they have been born again and are now kings and priests unto God through conversion and adoption (Rev. 1:6). They hold God to be their Father and Jesus Christ as their Saviour. These verses in 1 Peter speak of the priesthood of all believers. This is why both men and women are accepted before God in worship and why they are permitted to worship together, for God sees them as one body in Christ (1 Cor. 12:12–14).[16]

The New Testament is unwavering: only through Jesus Christ can worship be accepted by God Almighty. The Scriptures say, 'I am the way, the truth, and the life. No one comes to the Father except through Me' (John 14:6); 'Nor is there salvation in any other, for there is no other name under heaven given among men by which we must be saved' (Acts 4:12); '[God] has in these last days spoken to us by His Son' (Heb. 1:2).

There is no other Mediator but Jesus Christ, and no other way to God. This is what the Christian martyrs believed, and why they were willing to die.

There's no greater name than Jesus,
Name of him who came to save us;
In that saving name so gracious
Every knee shall bow.
(© Michael Baughen / Jubilate Hymns)

NOTES

1 Hadith narrated by Abu Said Al-Khudri (Sahih Bukhari 1:6:301), an authentic (*Sahih*) hadith; emphasis added.

2 Much of the rest of this chapter is based on 'Appendix 3: Prayer and Islam' in my book *Getting to Grips with Prayer: Its Realities, Challenges and Potential* (Leominster: Day One, 2017), pp. 137–142.

3 Jamaal al-Din Zarabozo, *The Friday Prayer, Part 1: The Fiqh of the Friday Prayer* (2nd edn; Ann Arbor, MI: Islamic Assembly of North America, 1998), p. 7.

4 'This is the Muhsen Khan Translation and the words in parentheses are not found in Arabic but are Muhammad's explanation taken from Hadith when they asked him who they were who had earned Allah's anger, and the answer was the Jews. Then they asked him, 'And who are those who went astray?', and the answer was the Christians. Other translators, like Yusef Ali, put that hadith in the footnote as an explanation. So every Sheikh knows what this prayer means but not every ordinary Muslim. But every Muslim who is educated in Islam knows that explanation' (Dr Berty Abdelmasih, in a personal email).

5 Stinted prayers are set liturgical prayers in prayer books.

6 The *Jewish* Prayer Book (*siddur*) *thanks* God for *not* making the Jew a Gentile, a slave or a woman. See 'Three Blessings', My Jewish Learning, http://www.myjewishlearning.com/article/three-blessings. Conversely, Christians give thanks that 'There is neither Jew nor Greek, there is neither slave nor free, there is neither male nor female; for you are all one in Christ Jesus' (Gal. 3:28).

7 Zarabozo, *The Friday Prayer, Part 1*, p. 5. I am indebted to Zarabozo for some of what follows.

8 In Abu Yahya al-Nawawi, *Sahib Muslim Bi-Sahib al-Nawawi*, Vol. 6 (Beirut: Dar al-Fikr, [n.d.]), p. 142. Zarabozo, *The Friday Prayer*, Part 1, p. 6.

9 *Ummah* = the whole body of Muslims worldwide.

10 This comment alludes to a historical incident when most of the congregation, on hearing that a long-expected trade caravan had come from Syria, rushed out of the mosque in the midst of Muhammad's Friday sermon. Muhammad Asad (trans.), *The Message of the Qur'an* (Bristol: Book Foundation, 2003), p. 986.

11 Albirr Foundation UK, *Salah: The Guide Book for Prayer* (London: Albirr Foundation UK, 2015), p. 9.

12 Albirr Foundation UK, *Basic Principles of Islam* (London: Albirr Foundation UK, 2015), pp. 21–26. I am indebted to this work for the information above.

13 See my book *Getting to Grips with Prayer*.

14 Herman Ridderbos, *The Gospel of John* (Grand Rapids, MI: Eerdmans, 1992), p. 121.

15 Albirr Foundation UK, *Salah*, pp. 4–5. However, the most important pillar is the first: the declaration of faith (the *shahadah*) which makes a person a Muslim. Prayer is second, but only to the *shahadah*. It is the most important way to worship, as opposed to fasting, giving alms, etc.

16 See 'The Priesthood of All Believers and Prayer' in ch. 5 of my book *Getting to Grips with Prayer*, pp. 57–61.

God is love

We have known and believed the love that God has for us. God is love, and he who abides in love abides in God, and God in him. (1 John 4:16)

The Christian doctrine of the love of God is grounded on the fact that 'God is love' (1 John 4:8, 16). This in itself speaks of the Trinity, as 'Love is something that one person has for another person. If God was a single person, before the world was made, he was not love.'[1] The love of God as understood by the Scriptures is related to God's creation and His creatures and it is a most precious doctrine. To recognize this love of God and to love in return is the joy of our salvation.

God is not just the fountain and spring from which love flows, He is the origin of love, and all true love derives from Him, 'for love is of God' (1 John 4:7). Love, therefore, does not just flow from Him as if He were a conduit or channel, but is 'part and parcel' of the divine Being Himself. Love is His very essence. This means that God cannot exist without loving. He cannot but love. He is and ever has been love. Love could never be absent from His Being and actions. Think of the one true God Almighty, and you think of love. Love, therefore, like God Himself, is not created and never slumbers nor sleeps (see Ps. 121). Before the world was created, 'God is love', and at creation God said, 'Let Us make man in Our image', and so man was made from the dust of the ground and Eve from Adam's side (Gen. 1:26–27; 2:7, 18–25); and after creation, God 'sent His Son to be the propitiation for our sins' (1 John 4:10).[2] By these miraculous works is God's eternal love made known: 'In this is love, not that we loved God, but that He loved us and sent His Son to be the propitiation for our sins.' This divine essence which is love[3] surpasses knowledge: oh, the height and length and breadth of it! Oh, its depth! It goes beyond understanding and is to be wondered at, embraced and enjoyed: 'everyone who loves is born of God and knows God' (1 John 4:7).

Islam

What does Islam say about the love of God? One writer says,

The Koran does not contain any passage which comprises any kind of systematic description of the character of God. In Arabic he is called Allah, which means simply 'The God'. God does not introduce himself in the Koran, as he does in the Old Testament . . . he remains . . . a mystery . . . A Muslim believer only knows the names of God, the attributes described in the Koran, and his dealings with mankind.[4]

Love as understood in Islam is a reciprocal affection, and this implies the equality of lover and beloved. For this reason a relationship with God is impossible. This idea of God's transcendence is not foreign to Christianity but through Jesus Christ God has found a way for His creatures to experience His love personally in the soul: 'We love Him because He first loved us' (1 John 4:19). The fact that we desire to be loved by others is a proof that men and women are made in God's image (Gen. 1:28).

Law of love

The Scriptures make it clear that God wants to be loved by us. The greatest priority in true religion is to love God our Father in heaven; Jesus Christ has made that clear: 'The first of all the commandments is: "Hear, O Israel, the LORD our God, the LORD is one. And you shall love the LORD your God with all your heart, with all your soul, with all your mind, and with all your strength." This is the first commandment' (Mark 12:29–31). When Jesus said, 'Hear, O Israel, the LORD our God, the LORD is one', He was quoting the *Shema* from Deuteronomy 6:4 (it is so called because the first word in the sentence in Hebrew is *Shema*—'Hear'). Ever since the

Shema was first spoken around 3,500 years ago, Hebrew theology has been monotheist. It is true that God revealed Himself as the one and only true God to Abraham around 4,000 years ago (Gen. 12). Indeed, monotheism did not originate with the Zoroastrians, as some claim, but in the Garden of Eden, as the Old Testament makes clear (Gen. 3:8–9).

To love God and our neighbour were the two thoughts which summed up the whole law of God in Moses' day and also in ours. The Jews were taught to love their neighbours (Lev. 19:18), and Christians have sought to follow this too. Personal love for God was a constant refrain in Moses' words to Israel—'I command you . . . to love the LORD your God, to walk in all His ways, and to hold fast to Him' (Deut. 11:22)—and this finds an echo in the Gospels and New Testament epistles, and is foundational to the Christian understanding of God.

God's Word and the ministry of Christ give insight into how the people of God are to handle the Decalogue and to view the relationship between law and grace. The following things are obvious:

THE LAW OF LOVE IS THE WHOLE DUTY OF MEN

When Moses brought down from Mount Sinai the two tablets of the law with the Ten Commandments inscribed on them, they revealed what God required of all Israel. They formed part of His covenant with them. These commandments were not only for Israel but are to be seen as the basis for all moral laws in human society. The Jews called them the 'Ten Words'. They were written by the hand of God and given to Moses, the leader of Israel, on Sinai on tablets of stone. It is often assumed that the first tablet contained commandments one to four and the second tablet the remaining six.[5] In the first five books of the Law in the Old Testament (the Torah) God taught His people through Moses that they were to love Him. Moses, in Deuteronomy, made a point of stressing this requirement to love God:

Chapter 3

Hear, O Israel: The LORD our God, the LORD is one! You shall love the LORD your God with all your heart, with all your soul, and with all your strength. (6:4–5)

What does the LORD your God require of you, but to fear the LORD your God, to walk in all His ways and to love Him. (10:12)

Therefore you shall love the LORD your God, and keep His charge, His statutes, His judgments, and His commandments always. (11:1)

I command you today to love the LORD your God, to walk in His ways, and to keep His commandments, His statutes, and His judgments. (30:16)

To love God our Creator and Father is the duty of all people everywhere in all ages. We are to love God first and always, with all our heart, soul, mind and strength, and our neighbour as ourselves. That God wants to be loved startles and surprises the non-Christian; it is the last thought on their mind and the last thing they are willing to do. Islam has no sense of this profound and wonderful reality in its theology or subjective experience.

THE LAW OF LOVE HAS ETERNAL VALIDITY

Loving God is something that has eternal validity, that is, it has unending legitimacy. This law will never be replaced (Rom. 13:8–9). We also have the Apostle James's teaching, 'If you really fulfill the royal law according to the Scripture, "You shall love your neighbor as yourself," you do well' (2:8). James goes on to call this the 'law of liberty' (2:12). So we see that the *Shema* was not only for *then*, it is also for *now*. It was not only for *them* (Jews), it is also for *us* (Gentiles—Christians, Muslims and others). It is not temporary but an unchanging commandment. There is a duty to love God and there is a joy in loving Him. This is expressed in the Shorter Catechism question 1:

Q. What is the chief end of man?

A. Man's chief end is to glorify God, and to enjoy Him for ever.

We read in the Acts that the gospel was to be preached first to the Jews and then to the Gentiles. This is what Paul did:

He said to me, 'Depart, for I will send you far from here to the Gentiles.' (Acts 22:21)

God was manifested in the flesh, justified in the Spirit, seen by angels, preached among the Gentiles. (1 Tim. 3:16)

For I am not ashamed of the gospel of Christ, for it is the power of God to salvation for everyone who believes, for the Jew first and also for the Greek. (Rom. 1:16)

The Messiah's truth and ministry is not limited to His own people, the Jews, but under the New Covenant He is to be proclaimed as the Saviour of the world—to Greeks, Chinese, Arabs, Africans, Saxons, Francs and Romans, and so on. This is because the prophetic word and gospel calls on *all* to repent: 'these times of ignorance God overlooked, but now commands all men everywhere to repent' (Acts 17:30).

THE LAW OF LOVE IS NOT LEGALISM (HOW COULD IT BE?)

This summery of the law given by Jesus Christ in Mark 12:29–31 is the greatest of all commandments and cannot, by any stretch of the imagination, be regarded as legalism. Legalism is what the Pharisees and ancient Jewish rabbis of Israel were concerned with when they carried on their lengthy debates about what the Ten Commandments meant in everyday life. They argued about whether one was greater or smaller in importance. Islam advocates something similar when it seeks to distinguish between the earlier and later sayings of Muhammad in the

Quran and the Hadith.[6] Legalism was what the Pharisees encouraged when they found 613 commands (248 positive and 365 negative) in the Old Testament. Here are the words of Jesus Christ regarding their ministry: 'Woe to you, scribes and Pharisees, hypocrites! For you pay tithe of mint and anise and cummin, and have neglected the weightier matters of the law: justice and mercy and faith. These you ought to have done, without leaving the others undone. Blind guides, who strain out a gnat and swallow a camel!' (Matt. 23:23–24).

To save us majoring on the minors and becoming doctrinaire like the Jewish scribes of old, the Saviour has given us a clear priority above all others. As J. C. Ryle said, 'A rule like this [the law of love] includes everything. It makes all petty details unnecessary. Nothing will be intentionally lacking when there is love.'[7] This is the opposite of legalism. This teaching is universal in Christian theology and practice: 'For you, brethren, have been called to liberty; only do not use liberty as an opportunity for the flesh, but through love serve one another. For all the law is fulfilled in one word, even in this: "You shall love your neighbor as yourself"' (Gal. 5:13–14).

THE LAW OF LOVE IS COMPREHENSIVE AND COMPLETE
Jesus tells us that love
  • Comes from the *heart*, which contains words and thoughts;
  • Grips the *soul*, where the emotions dwell;
  • Fills the *mind*, where intellect, attitudes and dispositions are kept;
  • Demands all our *strength*, where energy and might are sourced.
Therefore, our love for God does not mean loving Him sometimes and growing cold at other times, but rather is for all times. Love for God is to reside in a warm heart, not sometimes, or most times, but at all times (see Ps. 62:8). Men must love what He loves and hate what He hates. How can we deny Him this love when He gave His only Son to die for us (John 3:16)? Our love will increase in knowledge and feeling when we

meditate on this love and its grace. Meditation on Jesus' cross and atoning blood draws from the sinner the prayers of repentance and increased love for God.

THE LAW OF LOVE IS THE GREATEST OF ALL COMMANDMENTS

Christ was asked what was the greatest commandment (singular), so he told us! There is none other like it or as great as it. And when we have put all the other commandments together, this one holds greater weight than them all combined. Ryle put it thus:

How striking of the Lord's description of the feeling with which we ought to regard both God and our neighbour! We are not merely to obey the one or to abstain from injuring the other. In both cases we are to give far more than this. We are to give love, the strongest of all affections and the most comprehensive. A rule like this includes everything.[8]

In 1 Corinthians 13:13 we read, 'And now abide faith hope, love, these three; but the greatest of these is love.' Why is love the greatest? It has to do with love's make-up, its nature and its kindness. Faith and hope receive, accept and take, while love gives, and gives, and gives again. So it is with God, who is the giver of every good gift: 'In this is love, not that we loved God, but that He loved us and *sent* his Son to be the propitiation for our sins' (1 John 4:10).

Love is patterned after God, for 'God is love' (1 John 4:8). We are to love God better than we love ourselves and with all the powers of the inner being. We cannot love Him too well or too much. We are to love our neighbour as ourselves. This extraordinary love leads us to the cross and flows out from the cross to others. To love God is the priority we are to recognize and implement as this is the greatest commandment of all.

Chapter 3

Can God's love take us to heaven?

The scribe who asked the question, 'Which is the first commandment of all?', drawing the response from Jesus that we have looked at, acknowledged that loving Almighty God 'is more than all the whole burnt offerings and sacrifice' (Mark 12:28, 33; cf. Micah 6:6–8). This is where King Saul failed (1 Sam. 15:22). This unnamed scribe, said Jesus, was not 'far from the kingdom of God' (Mark 12:34a). Why? Because he had respect for the Scriptures. He learnt from the Scriptures. He trusted the Scriptures. He let the Scriptures judge him. Unless we do likewise, we will remain lost. Jesus said we must decrease by becoming as little children: 'Assuredly, I say to you, unless you are converted and become as little children, you will by no means enter the kingdom of heaven. Therefore whoever humbles himself as [a] little child is the greatest in the kingdom of heaven' (Matt. 18:3–4).

Did this scribe feel love for God? Did he feel deeply? Was there affection for God? Did he love what God loves and hate what God hates? Such things are the *fruit* of conversion when the love of God is shed abroad in our hearts by the Holy Spirit (Rom. 5:5). We know that he was not 'far from the kingdom'; however, he would not be saved until he humbled himself as a little child before the Master's teachings. Love, as commanded here, brings life and joy. This shows us that true religion must be rooted in, immersed in, grounded in and guided by love. Only then will it flourish in the soul. This is because God's grace results in transformed living (1 Cor. 6:9–11; 2 Cor. 5:17). All other duties, religious or otherwise, are dependent on being filled with love for God and our neighbour. Let us grasp this fact. It is the reason for the cross work of Jesus Christ. Responding in faith with repentance to the death of Jesus Christ on the cross will result in loving God with all one's heart, soul, mind and strength.

GOD LOVES LOST SINNERS

The incarnation of Jesus Christ was how God communicated and made known His love for His world ruined by the fall. No greater act of love was possible. Love had a purpose, which came from (the perfection of) God's own nature.[9] The Father sent the Son to die in our place: this was forgiving love; the Father sent the Son to save us: this was atoning love. Love found a way to redeem our souls: 'not that we loved God, but that He loved us' (1 John 4:10). This was an act of (electing) love and infinite mercy. It is freely given, it is gratuitous, and it is ours for the asking. God shows love that is real. This is not theory or sentimentality: this love is freely offered in the gospel. It is given, not to creatures innocent and pure, but to rebels and transgressors of the law of God who, having believed the good news of the gospel, repent of their sins, trusting in the promise of forgiveness: 'If we say that we have no sin, we deceive ourselves, and the truth is not in us. If we confess our sins, He is faithful and just to forgive us our sins and to cleanse us from all unrighteousness' (1 John 1:8–9).

NOTES

1 C. S. Lewis, *Mere Christianity*, quoted in Robert Letham, *The Holy Trinity* (Phillipsburg, NJ: Presbyterian & Reformed, 2004), p. 444.

2 Propitiation is the act of atonement for the undeserving and law-breakers which resulted in the turning aside of God's holy wrath.

3 It also includes awesome holiness.

4 Christine Schirrmacher, *The Islamic View of Major Christian Teachings* (Bonn: Culture and Science, 2008), p. 25. I am grateful for her help in what follows.

5 The Puritan George Swinnock (1627–1673) wrote: 'The first commandment teacheth us the object of worship; the second, the matter of worship; the third, the manner of worship; the fourth, the time of worship.' *Works* (Edinburgh: Banner of Truth Trust, 1992), p. 222.

6 This allows Muslims to give priority to the older (mature) sayings of their prophet, even when that encourages violence.

7 J. C. Ryle, *Expository Thoughts on the Gospels: Mark* (London: James Clarke & Co., 1965), p. 262.

8 Ibid.
9 John Murray, *Redemption: Accomplished and Applied* (London: Banner of Truth Trust, 1961), p. 12.

The Bible

The words of the LORD are pure words,

Like silver tried in a furnace of earth,

Purified seven times. (Ps. 12:6)

If they do not hear Moses and the prophets, neither will they be persuaded though one
rise from the dead. (Luke 16:31)

Islam has its own three sources of authority: the Quran, the Hadith
and the records of Islamic history (Sunna). Muslims will, however,
try to convince enquirers that it believes in the Torah (*Tauraat*), the
Psalms of David (*Zaboor*) and the Gospels (*Injeel*) as well as the Quran.
Yet, if one was to hear more, Muslims would explain that they mean
something very different from what the Christian might expect from that
statement! 'Christians boast about the Gospels . . . but there is not a single
Gospel "according" to Jesus himself!'[1] However, 'It is all but certain that
the Quran did not come together as a single volume in the lifetime of
Muhammad.'[2] After Muhammad's death the Quranic manuscript that
was in the care of his wife Hafsa and other elements of the Quran were
gathered together to form a complete copy minus variants in dialects.
The original and the three copies that were made have not survived.
Western academic historians claim that the Quran's present form
originates from 'the third Islamic century'.[3] It should be noted that
'There are clear differences between many of the ideas of the early
Meccan suras and the later Madinan suras. Some verses of the Quran
advise Muslims not to use force while others enjoin violence' (Sura 9:5;
2:256).[4] Thus the Quran speaks with an uncertain sound and accounts
for the 'mixed messages' given by Muslims.

How the Bible came to us

Christians believe that the Bible came to us supernaturally through divine revelation: 'All Scripture is given by inspiration of God' (2 Tim. 3:16); 'holy men of God spoke as they were moved ['carried along'] by the Holy Spirit' (2 Peter 1:21). This revelation is ultimately about God and His Son (John 1:1; 17:8, 14, 17). The Old and New Testament texts were preserved and protected in the providence of God.[5] The Bible can be understood through the activity of the Holy Spirit in regeneration (1 Cor. 2:14). Being divinely inspired, whatever the Bible says, whether that teaching has to do with doctrine, history, science, geography, geology or any other discipline or knowledge, it is accurate and correct. J. I. Packer put it this way: 'What the Bible says, God says, without error.'[6] To reject the Bible as reliable therefore leaves one with the options of philosophy *per se* on the one hand or mysticism on the other in the search for God: a choice of accepting the mind of God (revealed religion) or the mind of men (human knowledge). Christians claim that the Bible is wholly true, revealing what God wants us to hear and believe. We need not be afraid to cross the gap between time and eternity because beyond is the promise of eternal comfort in Christ Jesus our Lord (John 10:27–28).

THE OLD TESTAMENT TEXT

The Masoretic Text of the Old Testament 'is a carefully annotated product of a centuries-long tradition throughout which the sacred words were meticulously guarded, copied and checked by Jewish experts'.[7] The finding of the Qumran[8] Dead Sea Scrolls in Israel by three Bedouin shepherds in 1947 confirmed that the text has remained pure and that the Septuagint (LXX), the translation from the Hebrew into Greek from the third century BC onwards, brings us very near to the original manuscripts. The internal and external evidence for divine inspiration is strong and is to be accepted over against arguments for supposed redacted and changed texts, which Islamic propaganda asserts. This integrity holds true in prophecy. The prophet was not to speak in the name of another god, nor was he to speak a word that was not true or would not be fulfilled (Deut. 18:1–5; 18:20–22). To attempt to discredit what God has said and done is extremely serious and unbelieving. The Word of God is to be believed and obeyed. Discerning the word of truth means distinguishing the divine truth from that of the false prophet (John 10:34–36; 17:17; 2 Tim. 3:16).

THE NEW TESTAMENT TEXT

'The New Testament documents are better-preserved and more numerous than any other ancient writings. Because they are so numerous, they can be cross checked for accuracy.'[9] There are thousands more New Testament Greek manuscripts than for any other ancient writing. The originals were written in the first century AD and the time between originals and copies is estimated to be 'less than 100 years'. Today there are 5,686 Greek manuscript copies of the New Testament in existence; this compares to 49 copies of Aristotle's writings (384–322 BC) and 643 copies of Homer's *Iliad* (written c.900 BC). 'In addition, there are over 19,000 copies in the Syriac, Latin, Coptic and Aramaic languages. The total supporting New Testament manuscript base is over 24,000.' At the same time, we have absolutely no ancient documents contemporary with the first century that contest the New Testament texts. 'Compare these time spans with the next closest, which is Homer's *Iliad*, where the closest copy from the original is 500 years later. Undoubtedly, that period of time allows for more textual corruption in its transmission. How much less so for the New Testament documents?'[10]

The New Testament autographs

The apostles of Jesus Christ were very special men. We have the record of their names in Mark 3:14–19 and Matthew 10:1–4. There were no women among the Twelve. They are defined by the Bible as those who had seen Christ in the flesh and were genuine witnesses to the resurrection (Acts

1:21–22). They were foundational to the church, which is built on their teachings (Eph. 2:20). Once a foundation is laid it need not be laid again, and if it is replaced, it is *not* the same building. This needs to be remembered, as there are some who would carelessly call themselves 'apostles' and superior 'prophets' to the Son of God.

Almost all biblical scholars agree that the New Testament documents were all written before the close of the First Century. If Jesus was crucified in AD 30, then that means the entire New Testament was completed within 70 years. This is important because it means that there were plenty of people around when the New Testament documents were penned—people who could have contested the writings. In other words, those who wrote the documents knew that if they were inaccurate, plenty of people would have pointed it out.[11]

The New Testament writers did not have self-originating ideas or look into the Jewish Scriptures for proof-texts; rather, it was as they remembered or re-read the Old Testament Torah and prophecies that the Holy Spirit gave them true light and explanation. As the Apostle Peter noted, 'no prophecy of Scripture is of any private interpretation, for prophecy never came by the will of man, but holy men of God spoke as they were moved by the Holy Spirit' (2 Peter 1:20–21). They continually refer to the Old Testament as Scripture, quoting it as the authority of God given in prophecy. It can be seen that certain Old Testament passages and themes keep recurring in the New Testament corpus. The writers were aware that they stood under the authority and testimony of Old Testament covenant documents which were sacred Scripture. The New Testament authors were men whose minds were open to the Holy Spirit's help. The ancient Old Testament texts proved to the New Testament writers that Jesus of Nazareth really did fulfil Bible prophecy, yet it was only after Pentecost and the work of the Holy Spirit through the new birth that they were anointed to write under divine inspiration in order that their contemporaries and their successors might not be ignorant as to God's purposes and plans in the life and death of Jesus the Messiah (John 17:5; 20:30–31). Thus the New Testament was written supported by the Old via the inspiration of the Holy Spirit (2 Tim. 3:16; 2 Peter 1:19–21).

THE SIXTY-SIX BOOKS

The matter of producing a complete Christian canon of sixty-six books was time-consuming, but at the Council of Carthage in AD 397 reference was made to the canon as we know it today, making it clear that it is 'what we have received from our fathers'.[12] It relied on earlier documents produced and letters written in the first or second century AD. These apostolic writings and the original autographs were collected and examined. As Brian Edwards says,

With one exception, all our New Testament books are found in either direct quotations or allusions in the writing of these 'apostolic fathers' up to the year AD 180. That single exception is 2 Peter. By around AD 150 the New Testament canon of Scripture contains all but four of the Christian NT canon. Unlike the Gnostic and other false literature, the church Fathers did not make up new sayings of Christ or the apostles.[13]

Recognizing that holy men were inspired by the Holy Spirit to write the God-breathed documents we now call the Scriptures (1 Tim. 3:16), the church closed the canon. Because of this recognition the sixty-six books hold an authority and power unique in all the earth because they are God's Word.

THE BIBLE AND ST PAUL[14]

There are some who think that Paul and not Jesus was the source of the Christian faith. However, Christians rigorously dispute this notion. But it is right to ask who *was* Jesus Christ and what was He really like? True Christians believe that the answers are found in the pages of the New Testament, for it is there that we find the historical Jesus.[15] We cannot accept a view of Jesus Christ that is in opposition to the Scriptures, nor can we accept that there is another Christ who is different from the one the New Testament describes. He is found in the Gospel narratives and in the New Testament epistles.

It is, of course, true that Paul wrote most of the New Testament letters and that this informs what Christians all over the world believe and teach about Jesus Christ. But the New Testament also contains the writings of Luke, John, Peter and others, and they all agree as to the question 'Who was Jesus Christ?' Paul's message does not disagree with that of his contemporaries. Paul's writings enlighten us, for he was taught the history of Christ by eyewitnesses, he was steeped in Old Testament doctrine and he had the Holy Spirit as his interpreter. Let us remember that:

- Paul was a scholar who possessed an extraordinary mind. He spent his life reading, learning and teaching. He was a linguist who was fluent in Hebrew, Aramaic and Greek. He studied Jewish law under Gamaliel, one of the great teachers of his day (Acts 22:3). Gamaliel held the title 'Rabban, our teacher', a higher title than 'Rabbi, my teacher', and we read in Acts 5:33–40 of how he intervened 'with a resounding speech' at the trial of Peter and the other apostles. So Paul was tutored and mentored by one of the greatest scholars and teachers of his day.
- Paul was also a Pharisee (it means 'a separated one'). There were about 6,000 in the days of King Herod. They studied the law and set it out in a way intended to help the Jewish people keep it correctly. He studied the Old Testament in great detail and knew its teaching, prophecies, content and the implications of it all in the context of Jewish teaching and tradition, especially regarding

the Messiah (Gal. 1:14). He was a 'Pharisee of the Pharisees', which meant that he was a strict upholder of the law and the Jewish traditions.

- Paul was a historian very familiar with the New Testament realities. He knew what Jesus taught because he had heard about the miracles of Jesus from Ananias and the disciples of Damascus after his conversion (Acts 9:19). He then talked with Peter and James the Lord's brother (Gal. 1:18). In that encounter he was to learn first-hand from eyewitnesses what Jesus did, said and what He was like. Paul's friends—John Mark (who came from Jerusalem), Barnabas ('a good man, full of the Holy Spirit and of faith', Acts 11:24) and Doctor Luke (who wrote the third Gospel)—no doubt told him what they personally knew of the man called the Christ. Thus Paul was very familiar with the teachings, parables and stories of Jesus that we find in the Gospels.

- Paul was inspired, being under the influence of the Holy Spirit. He was a man equipped and prepared by God through conversion to grasp the deep things of God, and under the influence of the Holy Spirit Paul brought together the Old Testament revelation about the Messiah and the first-century facts, reports and testimonies concerning Jesus of Nazareth. When he did so, he saw that they all pointed to the same Person, namely, the One promised and the One crucified.

We have seen that Paul went back to the Old Testament Scriptures to find out what God said and did. This revealed the way of salvation and reconciliation between God the Creator and humanity the creatures *then* in the Old Testament and *now* in the New Testament dispensation also (Rom. 3:21). In Romans 4:3, 7–8, Paul quotes from Genesis 15:6 and Psalm 32:1–2 to prove that the doctrine of the imputed righteousness of God unto justification was known in the Old Testament era: 'Abraham believed God, and it was accounted to him for righteousness' (4:3);

'Blessed are those whose lawless deeds are forgiven, and whose sins are covered; blessed is the man to whom the LORD shall not impute sin' (4:7–8).

All these things made Paul the ideal man to preach and write the truth as it is in Jesus Christ.

The Bible's authority[16]

Truth is not found in human reason or experience but in divine wisdom. Jesus cleared up any misunderstanding as to what truth really is; He said it is God's Word: 'Your word is truth' (John 17:17). This is to be understood as being the sixty-six books of the Old and New Testaments but not the apocryphal books—they form no part of the canon and have no authority in the church. The Bible is complete, and no addition need be made to it (Gal. 1:8–9; 2 Tim. 3:16; Heb. 1:2–3). There are no fresh truths of revelation to be discovered, whether in nature or in church history and tradition, which are not to be found in Scripture. Christian tradition has no authority over God's Word, nor does it hold equal status as a source of God's revelation to humankind, as otherwise this would subordinate Scripture to church tradition. Scripture is the ultimate and final authority beyond which there is no appeal. Its authority rests with God Himself. He is its source and originator, so it has power to command and power to require submission. Christianity is a religion of revelation.

The authority and sufficiency of the Bible was recognized by the Protestant Reformers and their successors who stated clearly that the integrity of the sixty-six books of the Scriptures was to be upheld. The following is a summary of the Westminster Confession of Faith, chapter 1, 'Of the Holy Scriptures':

The Bible is necessary because the light of nature and the works of creation and providence are not sufficient to reveal the true nature and will of God or to bring men to salvation through Jesus Christ (Heb. 1:1–2). The Bible's authority is not dependent on the church's testimony or dogmas for it possesses an innate and unique authority all of its own which is witnessed to by the Holy Spirit. The Bible excels in truth, wisdom and light; however, it is the inward illumination of the Spirit that seals its truth and authority by and with the Word in our hearts. The Scriptures as they now exist are sufficient to bring men to repentance and faith and must not be added to by new revelations or traditions of men. They can be understood by the learned and unlearned for salvation. The Spirit of God immediately inspired the autographs so that they can be read when translated into the vernacular for light and comfort and are meant to be the final arbitrator in all matters of religion. We understand and interpret the Scripture by Scripture and it alone is the judge 'by which all controversies of religion are to be determined, and all decrees of councils, opinions of ancient writers, doctrines of men, and private spirits, are to be examined'. (1.10)

The FIEC (Fellowship of Evangelical Churches) Statement of Faith declares:

God has revealed Himself in the Bible, which consists of the Old and New Testaments alone. Every word was inspired by God through human authors, so that the Bible as originally given is in its entirety the Word of God, without error and fully reliable in fact and doctrine. The Bible alone speaks with final authority and is always sufficient for all matters of belief and practice.

To treat the Word of God as inerrant is to assert the doctrine of inerrancy; this means that 'the Scriptures in their original autographs and properly interpreted will be shown to be wholly true in everything they affirm, whether that has to do with doctrine or morality or with the social, physical or life sciences'.[17] D. M. Lloyd-Jones noted, 'We must believe the history of the Bible as well as its didactic teaching. Failure here is always an indication of a departure from the true evangelical position . . . We must assert that we believe in the historicity of the early chapters of Genesis and all other Biblical history.'[18]

Word and Spirit

God deals with us as rational creatures—with minds, wills and consciences. His Word enlightens the mind and gives understanding (Eph. 1:18). It is this truth accompanied by the power of the Holy Spirit that saves (He is called the Spirit of truth, John 16:13). The Holy Spirit is the agent of conversion working through God's Word to give light and guidance (2 Cor. 3:17–18; 1 John 2:27). The central position of English Puritanism was that 'the Spirit speaks in, by, or through the Word'.[19] Both the Word and the Spirit are necessary to inner growth in grace. So we can state: Bible truth plus the Holy Spirit equals Christian salvation. For John Calvin it was the Spirit of God that brought assurance to the soul: 'We have no great certainty of the word itself, until it be confirmed by the testimony of the Spirit. For the Lord has so knit the certainty of his word and his Spirit that our minds are duly imbued with reverence for the word when the Spirit shining upon it enables us there to behold the face of God.'[20]

The Christian apologist Francis Schaeffer wrote, 'There are two reasons in our day to holding to a strong uncompromising view of Scripture. First and foremost, this is the only way to be faithful to what the Bible teaches about itself, to what Christ teaches about Scripture, and what the church has consistently held throughout the ages.'[21] Evangelical Protestants believe that the Bible, 'being immediately inspired by God and kept pure in all ages', is the final appeal in all controversies, spiritual and temporal.[22] This is because the Scriptures of the New Testament are documents based on contemporary eyewitness statements and the apostles (Luke 1:1–4). They are also an exposition of the teachings of Jesus backed up by the Old Testament's clear self-revelation of God to the world, together with messianic predictions by the holy prophets. Islam's rejection of the integrity and inerrancy of the Bible has led it to reject its authority and sufficiency in all things that are holy, spiritual and true about the nature of God and the way of salvation through the incarnate life, death and resurrection of Jesus of Nazareth. It prefers its own holy book, the Quran, placing it above the Christian Scriptures in truth, reliability and authority. Islam says that the Bible is corrupted and cannot be trusted but that the Quran is an exact copy of the true Quran in heaven and 'perfect, intact, word for word, syllable for syllable, as first revealed to Muhammad'.[23] To discredit the integrity of the Bible's sixty-six books Islam, holding to a 'Theory of Corruption', teaches its followers that the Quran alone is the word of God (Allah).[24]

NOTES

1 Ahmed Deedat, *Is the Bible God's Word?* (Durban: Islamic Propagation Centre Internatinal, 1989), p. 8.

2 Peter G. Riddell and Peter Cotterell, *Islam in Conflict: Past, Present and Future* (Leicester: IVP, 2003), p. 58.

3 Ibid., p. 59, n. 5. The oldest existing complete copies are possibly the Kufic and Topkapi manuscripts dated to the early eighth century, and the Samarkand Kufic Quran, which dates to between AD 795 and 855.

4 Ibid., p. 61.

5 Copies of Scripture autographs were found by Erasmus of Rotterdam in 1516 and they along with later finds allow us to have the twenty-seven books of the New Testament today. 'Just as the Masoretic Text, compiled from the seventh century AD, formed the basic text of our Hebrew OT, so the *Textus Receptus* (or Received Text) compiled in the sixteenth century AD . . . formed the basic text for our Greek New Testaments.' Brian H. Edwards, *Nothing But the Truth* (Darlington: Evangelical Press, 2006), p. 257.

6 J. I. Packer, *God Has Spoken: Revelation and the Bible* (London: Hodder & Stoughton, 1985), p. 28.

7 James C. VanderKam, *The Dead Sea Scrolls Today* (Grand Rapids, MI: Eerdmans, 1994), p. 123.

8 Qumran is on the north side of the Dead Sea.

9 I am indebted for the following section to Matt Slick, 'Manuscript Evidence for Superior New Testament Reliability', Christian Apologetics & Research Ministry (CARM), 12 October 2008, http://carm.org/manuscript-evidence, reproduced in Appendix 4.

10 Ibid.

11 Ibid.

12 Brian H. Edwards, *Why 27?* (Darlington: Evangelical Press, 2007), p. 126.

13 Ibid., pp. 105–106.

14 This section is adapted from my book *Opening Up Colossians and Philemon* (Leominster: Day One, 2006), pp. 12–15.

15 There are other extant sources originating around the first and second centuries AD which speak of Jesus Christ. However, only in the pages of the New Testament do we find His true identity.

16 We will look at this further in the next chapter.

17 Paul D. Feinberg, 'The Meaning of Inerrancy', in Norman L. Geisler (ed.), *Inerrancy* (Grand Rapids, MI: Zondervan, 1982), p. 294.

18 D. M. Lloyd-Jones, *What Is an Evangelical?* (Edinburgh: Banner of Truth Trust, 1992), [page not known].

19 G. F. Nuttall, *The Holy Spirit in Puritan Faith and Experience* (Chicago: University of Chicago Press, 1992), p. 33.

20 J. Calvin, *Institutes of the Christian Religion* (Grand Rapids, MI: Associated Publishers and Authors Inc., [n. d.]), 1.ix.3, p. 38.

21 Francis Schaeffer, *The Great Evangelical Disaster* (Eastbourne: Kingsway, 1984), p. 46.

22 The Westminster Confession of Faith (1647); also the Baptist Confession of Faith (1689) and the Congregational Savoy Declaration of Faith and Order (1658): Chapter 1.

23 Steven Masood, *The Bible and the Qur'an: A Question of Integrity* (Carlisle: Paternoster/ Authentic Lifestyle, 2001), pp. xvi–xvii.

24 Ibid.

The Bible and truth

Your word is truth. (John 17:17)

The New Testament was given in order that we might believe 'His story': 'And truly Jesus did many other signs in the presence of His disciples, which are not written in this book; but these are written that you may believe that Jesus is the Christ, the Son of God, and that believing you may have life in His name' (John 20:30–31). As we saw in the last chapter, it was given as a reliable historical document made up of eyewitness accounts of those who knew Jesus Christ or who researched His life shortly after His death, resurrection and ascension (Luke 1:1–4; 4:22; John 1:14; 1 Cor. 15:3; Gal. 1:18–19 [Paul spoke to eyewitnesses]; 2 Peter 1:16–21; 1 John 1:1–4). The eyewitnesses were divinely chosen and were with Christ from the beginning. They were promised the assistance of the Holy Spirit to write clearly and truthfully (2 Peter 1:20–21) so that what others read is the truth about the historical Jesus Christ. God desires that the world might know about Christ and believe in Him and His saving work (John 3:16; 14:26; 15:16, 26–27; 16:13–15; 17:18; 20:21–22). History records no Christ other than the one presented to us in the New Testament (Acts 4:12).

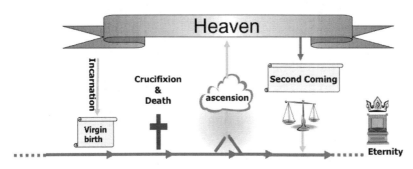

'HIS STORY' TIME LINE 1: THE CHRISTIAN VIEW

Chapter 5

External and internal evidence for the integrity of the Bible

The Bible text assures us that it is authentic. It comes from God and calls for trust in its integrity, authority and sufficiency unto salvation. There was given to men a gradual unfolding of revealed truth and knowledge. To some, as to Adam, God spoke directly (Gen. 3:9); to Abraham God spoke in visions (Gen. 12:1–3; 15:1; 18:1; 22:1ff.; etc.); to righteous Lot by angels (Gen. 19:1ff.); to Moses 'face to face' (Exod. 3:2; 4:2; 7:1ff.; etc.); to others, too numerous to record, by dreams and utterances through the prophets. Over a period of 1,500 years God engaged with His people and proclaimed His Word and truth to the Jews first. This climaxed with the coming of Jesus the Promised One:

God, who at various times and in various ways spoke in time past to the fathers by the prophets, has in these last days spoken to us by His Son, whom He has appointed heir of all things, through whom also He made the worlds; who being the brightness of His glory and the express image of His person, and upholding all things by the word of His power, when He had by Himself purged our sins, sat down at the right hand of the Majesty on high ... (Heb. 1:1–4)

After Pentecost Jesus was preached to the Gentile nations also (Matt. 28:18–20; Acts 3:12–26; 4:8–12; 8:5, 26–38; 1 Tim. 3:16).

The chronology of the world is provided by the Christian Scriptures and is historically reliable.

The New Testament speaks of Pilate, the Roman governor of Palestine when Jesus was alive. We have recorded these words from Pontius Pilate's lips, 'Behold the Man!' (John 19:5), spoken to the crowd outside the hall of judgement. It is interesting to note that it was not until 1961 that archaeological evidence was uncovered that proved (to the world) the existence and historical identity of Pilate. A slab of stone was discovered with both his name on it and that of Tiberius, the Roman governor at the time of Christ's death (written in Latin).[1] This no longer needs to be proved. Even as far back as 1974, *Time* magazine acknowledged this: 'After more than two centuries of facing the heaviest scientific guns that could be brought to bear, the Bible has survived and is perhaps the better for the siege. Even on the critics' own terms—historic fact—the Scriptures seem more acceptable now than they did when the rationalists began their attack.'[2]

CHRONOLOGICAL DETAIL

Chronological detail is accurately recorded in the Christian Scriptures; for example, 'Arphaxad was born "two years after the flood" (Gen. 11:10), and Jacob was 130 years old when he went to Egypt (Gen. 47:28)'.[3] Dr Luke was very precise (historically and theologically) in his Gospel and in the book of Acts; this, along with the chronological data of Scripture, was one reason why the authority and integrity of Scripture were accepted by the early church. Another example of internal evidence for the integrity of the Bible is the age of Abraham when he fathered Isaac (Rom. 4:14). The chronological priority of Abraham before Moses, which, we find in Romans 4, demonstrates that the gospel is of free grace for transgressors and sinners, establishes that the 'Bible has a [historical] story-line' which gives the gospel consistency.[4] The external evidence is also strong. The 'final destruction of Jerusalem happened in the eleventh year of Zedekiah (2 Kings 25:2) and the nineteenth year of Nebuchadnezzar (2 Kings 25:8). Records of the Babylonian history enable us to date the event at 587/586 BC.'[5]

GENEALOGIES[6]

A genealogy is a list of personal ancestors; it is a technical term that means a family history or record of descendants. The Old Testament has many biblical time lines in the form of genealogies. One important genealogy deals with the line of descent from Adam to Noah (Gen. 5). Another lists the descendants of Noah (Gen. 10). The line from Shem to

Chapter 5

Abram (Gen. 11:10–32) and the list of Abraham's offspring (Gen. 25:12–34) are extremely important for the early history of the Israelites. The longest Old Testament genealogy contains a detailed list of persons from Adam to the time of Saul (1 Chr. 1–9). The house of David was traced back to Perez (Ruth 4:18–22), the son of Judah (Gen. 46:12). This was an important genealogy because of the promises of the prophets about the Messiah. Jesus Himself accepted the integrity of the Old Testament books. His references to them are numerous, and on *His* say-so we accept their validity and authority (Matt. 21:42; 22:29; 26:54; Mark 12:10; Luke 4:21; 24:27; John 5:39; 17:17).

Two distinct lists of the ancestors of Jesus are found in the Gospels of Matthew and Luke. They contain names of people whom most of us would want to hide if they were in our genealogy:

• Two men who had sex with their wives' handmaids;
• One man who slept with his daughter-in-law;
• A prostitute;
• Someone who killed the husband of a woman he'd got pregnant;
• A line of political leaders who split and destroyed Israel.

This reminds us that the gospel is not about claiming a physical link to a prophet, person or culture because God saves by grace through faith in Jesus Christ alone. Historical lineage and our parents are not the guarantors of our salvation; that is dependent on God's mercy, love and will (John 1:12–13).

The Gospel of Matthew's genealogy (1:1–17) provides the legal lineage from David through Joseph to Jesus, while the Gospel of Luke's genealogy (3:23–38) provides the physical lineage from David through Mary to Jesus. The Gospel of Matthew records Christ's descent from the patriarch Abraham, while the Gospel of Luke reverses the order, contrary to biblical tradition, and traces the ancestry of Jesus back through Joseph, David, and Abraham to Adam, the son of God. Matthew used the Greek translation of the Hebrew Old Testament (the Septuagint,

LXX) for his forty-two names and grouped them in three units of fourteen generations each, fourteen being a multiple of the biblically symbolic number seven. Luke catalogued almost twice as many names as Matthew (seventy-seven) and also used the number seven as a basis for organizing Christ's ancestors. Jesus' mother is not mentioned in Luke's genealogy.

These lists have been preserved by God in perpetuity to tell the world that Jesus is the Christ *and* also the Saviour of the world. Their purpose was to show:

- That Jesus Christ the Messiah was descended from the house of David;
- That Christ is the Saviour of all peoples, not just the Jews;
- The real nature of the Messiah as the divine Son;
- That Jesus was a historical person.

The genealogies of Christ in the Gospels show the way in which the details of our Lord's descent from the house of David have been preserved through the centuries. He was of kingly and priestly stock as accredited by God Himself. The Bible has been very carefully constructed, exactly as we would expect given that it was authored by God the Holy Spirit.

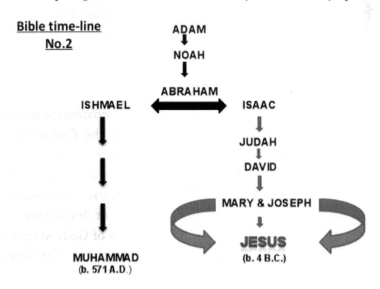

The Bible's genealogies do not include Muhammad, nor do they leave room for him; they flow from Adam, to Abraham, to Judah, to David, to Jesus Christ, and there they end. Because of this, Islam's aim is to discredit the integrity of the Bible and to destroy its message of the redeeming blood of the incarnate Son of God, Jesus Christ, who was born of Mary. However, both the New Testament and the Old Testament give us the clear message that Jesus Christ is the Prophet and Messiah of the church because of His virgin birth.

THE LORD OUR RIGHTEOUSNESS

For example, the Bible clearly demonstrates that Jesus fulfilled Old Testament prophecies of the Messiah and that He is God's Son and the way of salvation for us. He was not only Emanuel (God with us in person) but also the 'Branch' prophesied by Jeremiah who would become the righteousness of His people:

'Behold, the days are coming,' says the LORD,

'That I will raise to David a Branch of righteousness;

A King shall reign and prosper,

And execute judgment and righteousness in the earth.

In His days Judah will be saved,

And Israel will dwell safely;

Now this is His name by which He will be called:

THE LORD OUR RIGHTEOUSNESS.' (Jer. 23:5–6)

Notice what is said in the prophecy:
- This oracle from Jeremiah is about the future: '"The days are coming," says the LORD.'
- The king of whom Jeremiah speaks is a descendant of King David: 'I will raise to David a Branch of righteousness.' His lineage is through the seed of Israel (Jacob) and the tribe of Judah.

- This king is predicted to 'execute judgment and righteousness in the earth'. His reign is to be worldwide and his rule will be just, true and upright. This means that he has the power of an endless life.
- The contrast between this future king and David is seen in 'His name by which He will be called: THE LORD OUR RIGHTEOUSNESS.'
- This title, 'THE LORD OUR RIGHTEOUSNESS', is messianic as well as prophetic and declares that God's way of salvation for the world is through the righteousness that is by faith.

This prophecy refers to Jesus Christ, for there is a difference between the righteousness of Christ and King David. The contrast is deliberate and profound. Calvin says that the Branch 'executes righteousness, because he regenerates us by his Spirit. And he executes judgment because he bridles, as it were, the devil.'[7] Christ's kingdom on earth replaces all others and He rules with wisdom and grace (Ps. 121).

The prophet Isaiah's words add substance to those of Jeremiah:

There shall come forth a Rod from the stem of Jesse,

And a Branch shall grow out of his roots.

The Spirit of the LORD shall rest upon Him,

The Spirit of wisdom and understanding,

The Spirit of counsel and might,

The Spirit of knowledge and of the fear of the LORD.

His delight is in the fear of the LORD,

And He shall not judge by the sight of His eyes,

Nor decide by the hearing of His ears;

But with righteousness He shall judge the poor,

And decide with equity for the meek of the earth. (Isa. 11:1–4, emphasis added)

The Branch shall be assisted by 'the Spirit of the LORD', thus his wisdom, understanding, counsel and knowledge excel. The predicted 'Branch' shall be of the 'stock' (root) of Jesse the father of King David.

This future king would be of the family of David. Thus Jesus taught that He is 'the true vine' (John 15:1) and 'the Root and the Offspring of David' (Rev. 22:16). David's line had fallen into decay and we know that Jesus' mother was poor and insignificant; yet from that long-decayed root Jesus Christ would spring in fulfilment of these prophecies from Isaiah and Jeremiah. THE LORD OUR RIGHTEOUSNESS is the giver of peace with God; and it is faith in Christ Jesus that brings to the soul justification and both peace 'with' God and the peace 'of' God, without which we are lost eternally (Rom. 5:1).

The Apostle Paul, quoting from Isaiah 11 to express the days of the Messiah's coming—that 'There shall be a root of Jesse; and He who shall rise to reign over the Gentiles, in Him the Gentiles shall hope'—concludes, 'Now may the God of hope fill you with all joy and peace in believing, that you may abound in hope by the power of the Holy Spirit' (Rom. 15:12–13).

The Bible as truth
The power of God enlightens the soul and frees the will, producing faith and repentance, and bringing an internal witness to the believer that '[God's] word is truth' (John 17:17). Regeneration is the 'new birth' spoken of in John 3:5, 7 and is the New Testament's fulfilment of the prophecy in Ezekiel 36:25–27:

I will sprinkle clean water on you, and you shall be clean; I will cleanse you from all your filthiness and from all your idols. I will give you a new heart and put a new spirit within you; I will take the heart of stone out of your flesh and give you a heart of flesh. I will put My Spirit within you and cause you to walk in My statutes, and you will keep My judgments and do them.

The English Puritan John Owen listed eight rational external arguments for divine revelation:[8]

1. The antiquity of the writings of the Bible;
2. God's care and protection of the Bible;[9]
3. The design of the Bible: it is full of divine wisdom, it reveals God to man, it directs men to come unto the enjoyment of God;
4. That the Bible takes it on itself to speak for God;
5. That the Bible directs men to God to attain rest and blessedness;
6. The testimony of the church, which upholds the Scriptures and declares them (1 Tim 3:15). However, Owen says, 'We wholly deny that we received the Scripture from and on the authority of the Roman Catholic Church';
7. The success of the preaching of the Word: God's divine power accompanies the preaching of God's Word;
8. The uniqueness of the book: that is, the whole authority of the Scriptures in themselves depends solely on their divine original.[10]

THE KNOWLEDGE OF THE TRUTH

Those who believe are designated 'children of God' (1 John 3:1–2; John 1:12–13). How do the children of God know that Christianity is true? There is a role for evidence as well as for the work of the Holy Spirit. Reason under the guidance of God's Word and Spirit brings us to understand and believe. The message of the Bible is addressed to the mind and to the innate sense of God in the soul of man. When we speak of a sense of God in the soul we are saying that in the human consciousness 'there is implanted a *sensus divinitatis*, a *semen religionis* [a seed of religion], which impels it to seek after the knowledge of God'.[11] Thus the sinner is renewed and quickened by a special work of God's Spirit. It is in the Holy Scriptures of Christianity that God has provided the clearest and best testimony to Himself. Scripture is the only external means of divine supernatural illumination (Ps. 19:7–8; Isa. 8:20; 2 Tim. 3:15–17). God's Word contains all we need to know for salvation, and although there are many truths revealed in the Scriptures which in their own nature transcend human understanding, 'every essential article of faith and rule of practice may be clearly learned from Scripture'.[12]

WHAT IS TRUTH?

Islam plays with the truth. Its doctrine of *taqiyya* (dissimulation or concealment) allows deception in order to save face or honour or the reputation of Islam especially in times of religious persecution. Hamid Enayat, a Muslim historian who was a fellow of St Antony's College, Oxford, stated, '[*Taqiyya* has] in practice become the norm of public behavior among all Muslims—both Sunni and Shi'a—whenever there is a conflict between faith and expediency.'[13] This means that although 'truth' is considered very important to Islam and its religion, as revealed in the Quran, non-Muslims often face 'false or exaggerated statements introduced in order to make Islam appear in a better light'.[14] 'Islamization of knowledge' is 'part and parcel' of Muslim evangelization, and the Quran seems to justify this: 'And make not your own hands contribute to (Your) destruction but do good' (Sura 2:195).[15] Al-Bukhari narrated that Abu Ad-Darda' said, 'The Prophet Muhammad said, "We smile in the face of some people although our hearts curse them." Abu Hurairah and Jabir reported: The Prophet Muhammad said, "War is deception" (Bukhari and Muslim collections: Book 12, Hadith 1352). So if a Muslim consider himself to be at war with someone (or a nation), he is allowed to deceive them.

'What is truth?' was the question Pilot asked of Jesus in the Praetorium (John 18:38). He did not receive a reply because his question was meant rhetorically. Truth and not error is the means of holiness. 'Truth exists. It is real and absolute.'[16] However, it needs meaning. Christians believe that the Bible gives it meaning. Truth is timeless and trustworthy, so what we read in the Scriptures is to be believed. Christians believe that the Bible is true.

There is a distinction to be made between the light of nature and the light of the Word of God. Natural revelation displayed through creation shows us much about God, but it is not the truth that saves the soul. Nor are the general facts of history the means of greater holiness. If we say, 'The Prince of Wales married Lady Diana Spencer and they had two sons, Princes William and Harry', that does not make the slightest difference to the soul. However, if the Bible is read and believed it will work to the good of the soul. This means it must not be neglected. Truth transforms the fallen nature and makes it Christlike; 'Sanctify them by Your truth. You word is truth' (John 17:17).

THE VOICE OF GOD

The Word of God is the greatest and most effective instrument by which the Holy Spirit carries forward the work of salvation. The truth of the six-day creation of the world (Gen. 1–2)[17] and of the fall of Adam and Eve into sin (Gen. 3) has powerful and continued implications today, including the emphasis on a seven-day week with a weekly Sabbath rest. Without such truths there would be no gospel, and without the resurrection of Jesus Christ from the dead there would be no hope for lost sinners (John 20; 1 Cor. 15). It is this truth that justifies believers and makes them fit for heaven. The Bible is the revelation of God and of His Son for all mankind to believe. It is by listening to the voice of God through the Scriptures that men know how to live and how to die well. If we listen to the voice of Islam we might think we ought to accept all that is in the Quran as 'gospel'; however, God has revealed His will for mankind in the Ten Commandments and in all the pages of the Holy Scriptures (Exod. 20; Matt. 5–8).

NOTES

1 Ann Wroe, 'Historical Notes: Pontius Pilate—A Name Set in Stone', *Independent* online, 3 April 1999, https://www.independent.co.uk/news/people/historical-notes-pontius-pilate-a-name-set-in-stone-1084786.html.

2 *Time* magazine, 30 December 1974.

3 Stephen Lloyd, *Adam or Death* (Ely: Biblical Creation Trust, 2017), pp. 3–4.

4 Ibid., p. 4.

5 Ibid., p. 5.

6 I am indebted to *NKJV Study Bible* for help with this information (Nashville: Thomas Nelson, 1982).

7 J. Calvin, *365 Days with Calvin* (Leominster: Day One, 2008), 21 April.

8 John Owen, *The Works of John Owen*, Vol. 4 (London: Banner of Truth Trust, 1974), pp. 21–45.

9 'Owen's reasoning was as follows: If God gave the Bible to men, inspiring the very words in which it was written, surely he would preserve it in a substantially static form.' Sinclair Ferguson, *John Owen on the Christian Life* (Edinburgh: Banner of Truth Trust, 1995), pp.190f.

10 'He means Scripture's origin in God, not the original manuscripts or *autographa*.' Ferguson, *Owen on the Christian Life*, p. 185.

11 A. Kuyper, quoted in B. B. Warfield, 'Introduction to Francis R. Beattie's Apologetics', in *Selected Shorter Writings*, Vol. 2 (Phillipsburg, NJ: Presbyterian & Reformed, 1973), p. 96.

12 See A. A. Hodge, *The Confession of Faith* (Edinburgh: Banner of Truth Trust, 1987), p. 40.

13 Quoted in Patrick Sookhdeo, *Islam and Truth* (Pewsey: Barnabas Fund, 2013), p. 2.

14 Ibid., p. 4.

15 Ibid., p. 2.

16 Joan Bradly, *The Theory of War*, quoted in *The Times*, 24 January 2008.

17 These two chapters are not different views of the creation story; rather, Genesis 2 is an elaboration of Genesis 1's summary.

The virgin birth

And without controversy great is the mystery of godliness:

God was manifested in the flesh,

Justified in the Spirit,

Seen by angels,

Preached among the Gentiles,

Believed on in the world,

Received up in glory. (1 Tim. 3:16)

Mary (Maryam) the mother of Jesus is mentioned by name in the Quran, but stories are attributed to her therein which are not in the New Testament. A very different Annunciation narrative has the archangel Gabriel as a man—'a full-grown human being'—and the event (the seeding) hidden by Mary with a screen (Sura 19:17–21). Jesus is born underneath a date-palm tree (Sura 19:23).[1] It is worth noting that 'There are strong parallels generally between the Quranic account of Mary's life and the various Christian apocryphal writings'.[2] However, Islam is confused about Mary the mother of our Saviour, and it places her into what Muslims think Christians believe is the Trinity! The doctrine of the Trinity is aggressively rejected by Muslims both in the Quran and in their polemical writings. To them the doctrine of the Trinity is a blasphemy: 'They are deniers of the truth who say, God is one of three' (Sura 5:73). Nevertheless, Sura 5:116 makes out that Mary the mother of Jesus was seen as a god by some Christians. One writer talks of 'God, Jesus and Mary [as being] three gods and . . . the Christ [being] a child (*walad*) of God from Mary . . . and the trinity . . . a triad of Father, Son and Mother'.[3] Thus Christians are accused not only of being tritheists but also of lacking common sense![4]

Jesus Christ's incarnation by means of the virgin birth brought Him into the world as a man. He came in a special way because He was a special person and had a special purpose. He came, as Romans 8:3 says, 'in the likeness of sinful flesh' in order to condemn sin in the flesh; 'Therefore, when He came into the world, He said: "Sacrifice and offering You did not desire, but a body You have prepared for Me"' (Heb. 10:5). The Son of God, by means of the virgin birth, became man and took flesh and blood. This birth preserved His holiness as the sinless God and it produced His sinless humanity. He took human flesh and became Emmanuel, 'God with us' (Matt. 1:18–23). Jesus Christ was the God-man. The prophecy of Isaiah, 'For unto us a Child is born, unto us a Son is given' (Isa. 9:6), revealed that the Author of Christianity would be both human and divine, holding two natures together in one Person, and this was fulfilled in Jesus Christ.

The Apostles' Creed says that Christ 'was conceived by the Holy Spirit and born of the Virgin Mary'. This echoes the two incarnation narratives:

'Joseph, son of David, do not be afraid to take to you Mary your wife, for that which is conceived in her is of the Holy Spirit.' . . . So all this was done that it might be fulfilled which was spoken by the Lord through the prophet, saying: 'Behold, the virgin shall be with child, and bear a Son, and they shall call His name Immanuel,' which is translated, 'God with us.' (Matt. 1:20, 22–23)

And the angel answered and said to her [Mary], 'The Holy Spirit will come upon you, and the power of the Highest will overshadow you; therefore, also, that Holy One who is to be born will be called the Son of God.' (Luke 1:35)

Thus we have the authority of both Matthew and Luke on the subject of the virgin birth. The doctrine of the virgin birth is, of course, rejected by unbelievers and exaggerated out of all proportion by the cult of Mary the Virgin.[5] However, this must not stop us reading the sacred texts of the Bible on the subject. Remember that the virgin birth did not create the divinity of Jesus. He was always God begotten of the Father. It did not produce a demi-god: a half-God, half-human being. Only the God-man could atone for sin. Only the true Lamb of God can save us. This being so, the church has rejected lesser doctrines of Christ's Person and glory, such as the following:

- *Arianism*, which is held by the Jehovah's Witnesses today, was a fourth-century heresy. It was opposed by Athanasius of Alexandria[6] and rejected by the Council of Nicaea in AD 325. It sees our Lord Jesus Christ not in His New Testament clothes but as a creature created by God the Almighty and devoid of the deity and glory of eternal Sonship. Hebrews 1 answers this heresy.
- *Modalism* (Modalistic Monarchianism, also called Sabellianism and sometimes the Oneness Doctrine)[7] likewise threatens the truth about the Son. Here the Father becomes his own Son. Three different phases—manifestations—of God are said to be seen: 'the Father in creation, the Son in the incarnation and the Spirit in regeneration and sanctification'. This error is held by many Pentecostals today where it is known as 'Oneness Pentecostalism'.[8] This heresy is answered by John 16; Matthew 6; 1 Corinthians 8:6; and many other New Testament texts.

The Chalcedon Creed (AD 451) describes the orthodox position:

... our Lord Jesus Christ, at once complete in Godhead and complete in manhood, truly God and truly man, consisting also of a reasonable soul and body; of one substance (*homoousios*) with the Father as regards his Godhead, and at the same time of one substance with us as regards his manhood; like us in all respects, apart from sin.[9]

- *Apollinarianism* said that Jesus was incomplete man and incomplete God, being rather a mixture of the two. This meant that 'Christ had no human mind, soul will, or emotions, because the human psyche was replaced by his divine nature'.[10]

- *Docetism* (in the first century) questioned the reality of Christ's body. His body just seemed to be human. 'Of all the ancient heresies Docetism (or a form of it) is one which crops up most often in evangelicalism. F. F. Bruce says, "A weakness of the doctrine of our Lord's humanity . . . has been endemic in certain phases of the Brethren movement."'[11]

The incarnate Saviour was both man and God, having two natures. When the Word became flesh He never ceased to be God, not even for a moment. His deity was veiled (Phil. 2); 'the properties of each nature and substance were preserved entire, and came together to form one person'.[12] He came from eternity into time without losing his essential deity. The babe from Mary's womb was the 'only-begotten, recognized in two natures, without confusion, without change, without division, without separation'.[13]

Jesus' birth was the fulfilment of Old Testament prophecy

Being conceived by the Holy Spirit of God was the reality, and the virgin birth the sign.[14] The virgin birth did not transfer to Jesus a sinless perfection; His sinlessness was not because Mary was sinless[15] but because of 'a special divine work of preservation'.[16] This virgin birth was prophesied by Isaiah:

The LORD spoke again to Ahaz, saying, 'Ask a sign for yourself from the LORD your God; ask it either in the depth or in the height above.'

But Ahaz said, 'I will not ask, nor will I test the LORD!'

Then he said, ' . . . Therefore the Lord Himself will give you a sign: Behold, the virgin shall conceive and bear a Son, and shall call His name Immanuel.' (Isa. 7:10–14; the Hebrew for 'virgin' is *alma*, meaning an unmarried woman; cf. Matt. 1:23)

For unto us a Child is born,
Unto us a Son is given;
And the government will be upon His shoulder.
And His name will be called
Wonderful, Counselor, Mighty God,
Everlasting Father, Prince of Peace. (9:6)

Jesus' birth was history in the making

'This is not a human hypothesis, but a divine discourse. It was first a fact and then a doctrine.'[17]

The Holy Spirit will come upon you, and the power of the Highest will overshadow you; therefore, also, that Holy One who is to be born will be called the Son of God. (Luke 1:35)

[Christ Jesus,] being in the form of God, did not consider it robbery to be equal with God, but made Himself of no reputation, taking the form of a bondservant, and coming in the likeness of men. And being found in appearance as a man, He humbled Himself and became obedient to the point of death, even the death of the cross. (Phil. 2:6–8)

And the Word became flesh and dwelt among us, and we beheld His glory, the glory as of the only begotten of the Father, full of grace and truth. (John 1:14)

According to the New Testament, the 'Word' (*logos*) existed before He became flesh (John 1:1–3; 17:5). The virgin birth was the means by which God became man. The Son of God, without ceasing to be what He was—the Second Person of the holy Trinity—took body and soul into union with His divine nature to become Emmanuel, God with us. He was born without sin. His human mother did not contaminate Him with the guilt of Adam's first sin (Ps. 51:5; Rom. 5:12). He had a full and true humanity but without a sinful nature: 'Inasmuch then as the children have partaken of flesh and blood, He Himself likewise shared in the same' (Heb. 2:14). This was the reason for the virgin birth. The Holy Spirit effected Christ's supernatural conception. He also endowed Him with all that was necessary to be perfect man and to enable His humanity to develop in wisdom, and the grace of God was upon Him (Luke 2:40).

Jesus' birth had a purpose

Jesus, the incarnate Son, was sent to 'save His people from their sins' (Matt. 1:21). Jesus carried out every function of His messianic office in the power of the Holy Spirit (Isa. 61:1; Luke 4:17–19). The Spirit remained with Him, always controlling His mind, will and actions. As the holy Prophet of God, the Almighty, He declared the Word of God infallibly. As High Priest of the church, the Son of God made atonement for men by offering Himself without (personal) sin to God 'through the eternal [Holy] Spirit' (Heb. 9:14). He is also the King and Head of the church, ruling over it by the witness of the Holy Spirit to each believer (Heb. 10:15). Thus the virgin birth was essential to the work of redemption and to Christ's Kingship over His church for all ages. Only the God-man could atone for sin, and Jesus Christ was that One who alone was able to 'stand in the gap' and reconcile fallen humanity to the offended God of creation. C. H. Spurgeon could say,

The law was a dispensation of terror; the gospel draws with bands of love. The law repels, the gospel attracts. The law shows the distance which there is between God and man; the gospel bridges that awful chasm, and brings the sinner across it. With the sweet word 'Come' we are drawn to repentance and faith for forgiveness and peace with God.[18]

Only the true Lamb of God can save us. He became part of our human

history, intervening and coming to rescue us from the consequences of
the fall.

Down from His glory, ever-living story,
My God and Saviour came,
And Jesus was His name;
Born in a manger,
To His own a stranger,
A man of sorrows, tears and agony.[19]

Jesus' birth was a triumph

Jesus came at the right time in the history of the world. God sent His Son
on a mission of mercy and love clothed with humanity: 'when the fullness
of the time had come, God sent forth His Son, born of a woman, born
under the law, to redeem those who were under the law, that we might
receive the adoption as sons' (Gal. 4:4–5). This moment in history was
vindicated when by the Spirit's power at Pentecost the empowered and
energized believers took the gospel message to the whole world.

The Bible had foretold that God would send the 'Prince of Peace' to
His people in their troubles (Isa. 9:6–7), and the birth of Jesus Christ
fulfilled this prophecy. The life of the Son of God among us was the
consequence of the virgin birth. How wonderful is the account of the
heavenly choir of angels that sang to the shepherds to the glory of God on
the night of the birth of Christ, the world's Messiah: 'And suddenly there
was with the angel a multitude of the heavenly host praising God and
saying: "Glory to God in the highest, and on earth peace, goodwill
toward men!"' (Luke 2:13–14). Now we know why the Saviour came: to
make peace. God and sinners are now reconciled by His death: 'Having
been justified by faith, we have peace with God through our Lord Jesus
Christ' (Rom. 5:1). This is what we must believe. The Christ of the

Gospels with its genealogies and His words is the only Christ the world has. If it rejects Him, it rejects God's solution to the sin problem because Jesus Christ alone is the way, the truth and the life (John 14:6). The disciples of Christ saw and examined the majesty of His grace: 'we beheld His glory, the glory as of the only begotten of the Father, full of grace and truth' (John 1:14). Matthew 4:12–16, quoting Isaiah 9:1–2, says that Jesus

came and dwelt in Capernaum . . . that it might be fulfilled which was spoken by Isaiah the prophet, saying:
  'The land of Zebulun and the land of Naphtali,
  By the way of the sea, beyond the Jordan,
  Galilee of the Gentiles:
  The people who sat in darkness have seen a great light,
  And upon those who sat in the region and shadow of death
  Light has dawned.'

These chosen ones considered the mystery of His miracles and wonders and saw the attributes of His deity shining through the veil of His humanity. They were united in consciously accepting the evidence of His glory, and if you had been there you would have accepted Him as *your* Messiah too! The eleven apostles remembered the message of His love and declared Him to be the Light of the world:

What condescension,
Bringing us redemption;
That in the dead of night,
Not one faint hope in sight,
God, gracious, tender,
Laid aside His splendour,
Stooping to woo, to win, to save my soul.[20]

Islam accepts Jesus' virgin birth and acknowledges Him to be a sinless prophet, but insists that, though He was special, He was only a human being. To call Him 'Son of God' is, for the Muslim, blasphemy. Nevertheless, we have seen that the Scriptures set Him high above all others as the 'Child [who] is born' and 'a Son [who] is given' (Isa. 9:6). Without this there could have been no atoning reconciling work (propitiation) on the cross for sinners: 'He Himself is the propitiation for our sins, and not for ours only but also for the whole world' (1 John 2:2).

NOTES

1 The newborn baby Jesus speaks to Mary's relatives 'saying, "I am God's servant"' (Sura 19:29–30; 3:46).

2 Tom Holland, *In the Shadow of the Cross* (London: Abacus, 2013), p. 52 and p. 53, n. 74.

3 Zamakhshari on Sura 4:169, quoted in S. M. Zwemer, *The Moslem Doctrine of God* (American Tract Society; repr. Gerrards Cross: WEC Press, 1981), pp. 80–81. See Sura 5:116.

4 Some years ago, while teaching children the catechism, the author asked, 'In how many Persons does the one God exist?' When the question was then asked, 'Who are they?' a child from a non-Christian home answered, 'The Father, Jesus and the Virgin Mary'! The author has no doubt that this was because of the Roman Catholic Church's unbiblical views of the virgin Mary. Did Muhammad and his advisers/followers have the same impression in their day as that child did?

5 While we reject the Roman Catholic cult of the virgin Mary, which has been added for dogmatic reasons and takes away the glory due to Jesus, we thank God for Mary's faith and humility as a child of redemption.

6 Louis Berkhof, *The History of Christian Doctrines* (London: Banner of Truth Trust, 1969), p. 85. Berkhof says that Athanasius 'stands out on the pages of history as a strong, inflexible and unwavering champion of the truth'.

7 Ibid., pp. 78f.

8 *Dictionary of Pentecostalism and Charismatic Movements* (Grand Rapids, MI: Zondervan, 1995).

9 Council of Chalcedon, Actio V, Mansi vii.116f., as quoted in Henry Bettenson, *Documents of the Christian Church* (London: Oxford University Press, 1974).

10 F. F. Bruce, quoted in Jonathan F. Bayes, *The Apostles' Creed* (Eugene, OR: Wipf & Stock), p. 70.

11 Ibid., p. 69.

12 Bettenson, *Documents*, p. 50.

13 Council of Chalcedon, in Bettenson, *Documents*, p. 51.

14 Did God create an embryo and implant it in Mary's womb? See Bayes, *Apostles' Creed*, p. 64. This is done today by medical science in the process called *in vitro* fertilization.

15 The doctrine of the Immaculate Conception, defined by Pope Pius IX in December 1854 in the papal bull *Ineffabilis Deus*, teaches that Mary the mother of Jesus was, from conception, free from original sin.

16 Robert L. Reymond, *Systematic Theology* (Nashville: Thomas Nelson, 1998), p. 551.

17 H. Dermot McDonald, *Who Is the Real Jesus?* (McLean, VA: Isaac Publishing, 2012), p. 14.

18 Charles H. Spurgeon, *Morning and Evening*, 16 December (McLean, VA: MacDonald, [n.d.]).

19 William E. Booth-Clibborn (1893–1969).

20 Ibid.

The historical Jesus

And the Word became flesh and dwelt among us, and we beheld His glory, the glory as of the only begotten of the Father, full of grace and truth. (John 1:14)

Islam is not unprejudiced, unbiased or impartial when it comes to Christianity: it cannot tolerate the Christian worldview or permit errors in its own theology to be made known. Islam is convinced that it is Christianity that is seriously flawed and that Jesus Christ is not God the Son. It is written, 'Jesus in the sight of God is like Adam. He created him from dust' (Sura 3:59). All who deny this as the reality are therefore called 'liars' and are to be prayed against 'earnestly' and a curse of God invoked upon them, for 'there is no deity save Him [Allah]' (Sura 3:62). Islam also claims that the disciples of Jesus were Muslims: 'We are supporters of Allah and testify that we are those who are Muslims submitting to His will' (Sura 3:52)![1] These two statements from the Quran show that Islam rejects the New Testament as a reliable historical document made up of eyewitness accounts from those who knew Jesus Christ or researched His life before writing about it shortly after His death (Luke 1:1–4; John 1:14–18; Gal. 1:18–24; 2 Peter 1:16–21; 1 John 1:1–4). This rejection of Christ's deity is irrational. We think that sheer prejudice has blinded Muslims so that they will not accept the historical facts.

Not only the resurrection itself but also the day on which Christ rose from the dead—the first day of the week—proclaims Christ's glory and messianic mission. He rose on the third day and seven days later, on the first day of the week (called in Scripture the 'eighth day'), He appeared to eyewitnesses again, this time including doubting Thomas (John 20:26).[2] We cannot see Christ in His resurrected and glorified body for He is in heaven, nor were we at the resurrection event itself; but the eyewitnesses have recorded the facts for us in the inspired New Testament accounts. However, the Christian Lord's Day, every first day of the week, points fifty-two times a year to His triumph over death and Satan. This is a powerful witness to the mission of the churches and the gospel of Jesus Christ.

What do the Scriptures say about Christ?

For the truth about Christ Himself, we must turn to the Scriptures of the Old and New Testaments. It is there that we learn about the prophesised and historical Jesus and there that we see the glory of this One who was the object of so much anticipation. Jesus Himself claimed to be the 'sent one', and the biblical record testifies that He was the Son of God incarnate, the Messiah. Liberal Christianity perpetuates the lie that the Bible does not say that Jesus claimed to be divine, thus falsifying the Bible's record of the historical testimony of Jesus himself. The apostolic witnesses believed that He was indeed the Christ, the Son of the living God. In Caesarea Philippi, Jesus asked His disciples,

'Who do you say that I am?'

Simon Peter answered and said, 'You are the Christ, the Son of the living God.'

Jesus answered and said to him, 'Blessed are you, Simon Bar-Jonah, for flesh and blood has not revealed this to you, but My Father who is in heaven . . . on this rock[3] I will build My church, and the gates of Hades [hell] shall not prevail against it.' (Matt. 16:15–18)

All four Gospels were written in order that the world might know who Jesus Christ really is and what He came to earth to achieve. Ancient historians such as the Jewish Josephus (AD 37– c.100) and the Roman Tacitus (AD 56–117) acknowledged the historical existence of Jesus of Nazareth in their writings, but the Bible does more: it records Jesus' works of power, His atonement for sinners and His God-man nature

(John 1:14). In the opening chapter of John's Gospel various wonderful titles and names are given to our Lord Jesus Christ which elevate Him above all others:

- The Word (vv. 1, 14);
- The true Light (vv. 5, 7–8);
- Jesus Christ (v. 17);
- The only begotten Son (v. 18);
- The Lord (v. 23);
- The Lamb of God (vv. 29, 36);
- The Son of God (vv. 34, 49);
- Rabbi/Master (v. 38);
- The Christ (Messiah) (v. 41);
- Jesus of Nazareth (v. 45);
- The King of Israel (v. 49);
- The Son of Man (v. 51).

All this indicates that the person this Gospel speaks about is very special indeed.[4]

'I AM' SAYINGS

The 'I am' sayings of Jesus Christ are also recorded for us in the Gospel of John. There are eight in total:

- I am the bread of life (John 6:35, 48).
- I am the light of the world (John 8:12; 9:5).
- Before Abraham was, I am (John 8:58).
- I am the door (John 10:9).
- I am the good shepherd (John 10:11).
- I am the resurrection and the life (John 11:25).
- I am the way, the truth and the life (John 14:6).
- I am the true vine (John 15:1).

These are straightforward and clear summaries of Jesus' personal understanding of His messianic calling and office. They are singularly instructive of His messianic saving work. Together they combine to reveal the way to find God and enjoy Him forever.

It is clear from the Gospel accounts that Jesus had a strong sense of His calling and incarnate destiny. Those who say He did not know that He was the Messiah are not reading the text of Scripture with honesty or clarity of thought. Some make this claim out of a mistrust of Holy Writ and a sceptical, agnostic view of supernatural religion. While giving Jesus some recognition as a prophet of God and a teacher of righteousness (as we have seen), Islam fails to honour Him as the Redeemer of God's elect through grace. Islam's religious system of good works—the keeping of the 'Five Pillars of Islam'—is a legal obligation placed on all Muslims, and their salvation depends on their obedience that can only ever be imperfect; it is wholly works-based. The idea that salvation and acceptance with God the Almighty is based on works is rejected by the whole of the Old and New Testaments.[5] God's free grace is the Christian distinctive that outshines all apostate, false and cultic religion. It bestows salvation on those whom God has chosen from the foundation of the world, excluding works of merit by the gift of faith alone through Jesus Christ: 'I am the door of the sheep. All who ever came before Me are thieves and robbers, but the sheep did not hear them. I am the door. If anyone enters by Me, he will be saved, and will go in and out and find pasture' (John 10:7–9).[6]

Jesus is to be enjoyed by faith, so believers must embrace Him as the 'the bread of life', 'the light of the world', 'the good shepherd', 'the true vine', and so on. There was a time when He was before Abraham (John 8:58), which indicates not only His existence prior to creation but also His eternal Sonship (17:5). This makes Him without any doubt the 'door' into the eternal fold of God (10:9). The 'sheep' who trust that He is 'the way, the truth, and the life' (14:6) will at death be with Him in heaven and will at the last share in the hope of the resurrection to come. This is because He alone is 'the resurrection and the life': 'I am the resurrection and the life. He who believes in Me, though he may die, he shall live. And whoever lives and believes in Me shall never die. Do you believe this? (11:25–26).

THE WORD BECAME FLESH

There was always something special about the man Jesus Christ, and John's Gospel tells us why:

The Word became flesh and dwelt among us, and we beheld His glory, the glory as of the only begotten of the Father, full of grace and truth ... And of His fullness we have all received, and grace for grace. For the law was given through Moses, but grace and truth came through Jesus Christ. No one has seen God at any time. The only begotten Son, who is in the bosom of the Father, He has declared Him. Now this was the testimony of John ... (1:14, 16–19a)

This statement echoes John 1:1–2: 'In the beginning was the Word, and the Word was with God, and the Word was God. He was in the beginning with God.' The Greek word *logos* is the same in both verses, literally 'God was the Word'. 'The Word was God' is a good translation of the Greek text. As Hendriksen says, 'The predicate precedes the subject to emphasize Christ's full deity.'[7] These words speak of Jesus Christ's eternal Sonship. He was already the only begotten before His incarnation by eternal generation (Isa. 9:6a; John 17:5). He always was and will be the Word (*logos*), and as the Word, Jesus always existed (John 1:15). The Unitarian doctrine—that is, the doctrine of the Arians, who historically denied the doctrine of the Trinity from the fourth century AD—is similar to Islamic denials. It denies the divinity of Jesus Christ and His co-equality with the Father and the Holy Spirit. John's words tell us that Christ was the Son before the incarnation. His genealogy in the Bible goes back to God: ' ... son of Adam, the son of God' (Luke 3:38). Eternally begotten, the Christ was always the everlasting Son:

Chapter 7

I will declare the decree:
The LORD has said to Me,
'You are My Son,
Today I have begotten You.' (Ps. 2:7)

For to which of the angels did He ever say:
   'You are My Son,
   Today I have begotten You'?
And again:
   'I will be to Him a Father,
   And He shall be to Me a Son'? (Heb. 1:5)

But when the fullness of the time had come, God sent forth His Son, born of a woman, born under the law, to redeem those who were under the law, that we might receive the adoption as sons. (Gal. 4:4–5)

He came from eternity into time without losing His essential deity. It is not accurate to say '*Jesus* became flesh'; this name was given to Him after His incarnation. Nor is it right to say, '*Christ* became flesh', because Christ is the product of the incarnation, that is, God and man in one Person. Thus we read that the 'Word [*logos*] became flesh and dwelt among us' (John 1:14). At the incarnation and appearing of the Messiah the Logos united with human nature (and that without sin), but neither swallowed up the other. His divinity was not laid aside; He remained perfect God and became perfect man. These two natures were not confounded but remained unmixed and distinct. Thus we read,

And without controversy great is the mystery of godliness:
   God was manifested in the flesh,
   Justified in the Spirit,
   Seen by angels,

Preached among the Gentiles,
Believed on in the world,
Received up in glory. (1 Tim. 3:16, emphasis added)

Jesus Christ's incarnation is shown in type in the Old Testament when we consider the tabernacle. There God promised to meet with His people. It had specially designed furnishings and fittings intended to point to the Messiah to come. One special piece was the Ark of the Covenant which housed the Ten Commandments written on the two tablets of stone. It resided in the Holy of Holies behind the veil. The Ark was made of wood overlaid with pure gold. It represented our Saviour and was sprinkled with sacrificial blood on the Day of Atonement (*Yom Kippur*) for forgiveness of sins. These two materials—gold and wood—represented Christ's deity and humanity. They were not mixed or mingled; they remained 100 per cent wood and 100 per cent gold, but were used together to make one holy object wherein the law of God was placed. Likewise, Jesus Christ is 100 per cent God and 100 per cent man in one Person and the law was written on His heart. The Ark thus pointed forward to Christ's incarnation. Nothing of the essential nature of deity was lost in this event. John uses the word 'flesh' to refer to our physical nature not to our sinful disposition. Jesus chose to come into the world in human form and dwell among us. The Greek word translated 'dwell' comes from the word for 'tent' that was used in the Greek version of the Old Testament (LXX) for the tabernacle, where the presence of God dwelt. Christ's body was the tent in which deity lived for thirty-three years. That the disciples 'beheld His glory, the glory as of the only begotten of the Father, full of grace and truth' (John 1:15) speaks of the mystery of revelation which was and still is the theme and central doctrine of the gospel, namely, that

[Jesus,] being in the form of God, did not consider it robbery to be equal with God, but made Himself of no reputation, taking the form of a bondservant, and coming in the likeness of men. And being found in appearance as a man, He humbled Himself and became obedient to the point of death, even the death of the cross. (Phil. 2:6–8)

THE HUMANITY OF JESUS CHRIST

History records a human Christ with bodily needs and blood flowing in his veins. While remaining fully God in order to save us (Acts 20:28), the incarnate Jesus took human nature in the womb of the virgin Mary and became perfect man. Through union with us He greatly dignified our human nature while always remaining fully God. Because our Saviour is God and man in one Person, the New Testament tells us that He understands us (Heb. 4:15). He was a real person with a human body and soul, but He had a temporary presence in the world.

THE GLORY OF JESUS' PERSON

John said, 'We beheld His glory' (John 1:14). To 'behold' is to observe, not just to glimpse but to take a good look, and this resulted in a reasoned conclusion about who Jesus really was—not just by John, but among all eleven apostles. They saw His glory: they considered it, reflected on it, examined it carefully and marvelled at it. They saw and considered the mystery and majesty of His works. Because of their three years with Jesus of Nazareth they could observe the attributes of His deity shining through the veil of His humanity. They did not accept His teaching and His resurrection irrationally; rather, their minds and hearts were awakened by His Spirit to understand His revealed glory. Thus there was no bewitching or deluding, but they savingly believed, consciously accepting all the evidence of His messianic ministry.

The phrase 'full of grace and truth' (John 1:14) speaks of His divine and human attributes, exclusive to Jesus Christ the God-man. This is what John and the others saw when they lived with Jesus Christ. Thus John tells us that the Word who became flesh is unique.

THE CHRIST'S TWO NATURES

Jesus Christ is 'the image of the invisible God' (Col. 1:15), not just because He is perfect man as made in the image of God (Gen. 1:26–27; 1 Cor. 11:7) but because He has the same nature as God (Heb. 1:3), being co-eternal with Him (see next chapter). The Father is invisible to us, but God had made Himself known to us by His Son (John 14:9). Jesus Christ is eternally God's image and in Him the invisible God has become visible. He pre-existed with the Father before the world was created as 'the firstborn over all creation' (Col. 1:15), being the Father's heir (Rom. 8:29; 1 Cor. 15:20; Col. 1:18; Heb. 1:6; Rev. 1:5). 'With reference to his divinity, in which he has no brothers, the Son is called "only-begotten" (*unigenitus*), but with reference to his humanity, in which he is qualified to have brothers, he is called "first-begotten" (*primogenitus*).'[8] The undivided union of the two perfect natures in Christ gives infinite value to His atoning work on the cross and fits Him to be the Mediator between God and man. Because of this union:

- He sympathizes with us.
- He deals with the Father on our behalf on equal terms.
- His atoning blood has eternal value.
- He supplies a righteousness which has infinite value and by faith is imputed to sinners.
- He is our perfect example.
- He has dignified humanity.

THE MIRACLES OF JESUS

The canonical Gospels agree that Jesus' signs and wonders declared His glory, grace and love for sinners who were ruined by the fall. These supernatural works witnessed to His nature as God incarnate who dwelt among us in the flesh. He became part of our human history, intervening to rescue us from the consequences of the fall into sin.

Chapter 7

Conclusion

Islam considers Jesus Christ to be one of the ongoing series of prophets of Allah with special reference to the Jews (Sura 6:85). He was sent because the Jews had deviated from the teachings of Moses and the other Old Testament prophets. However, Jesus Christ was God and man, divine and human, possessing all the essential qualities of both the human nature and the divine. T. C. Hammond noted, 'while the two natures were united, they were not intermingled and altered in their individual properties.'[9] This doctrine sparked off the longest and fiercest controversy in the history of the church. The opposition was known as Arianism, from Arius, a presbyter of a church in Alexandria, who said that God, because He is unique, transcendent and invisible, cannot be shared or communicated (see previous chapter). Islam has chosen to follow Arius rather than Athanasius (the historic defender of the doctrine of the Trinity). So Islam makes out that Jesus Christ

- Was created out of nothing;
- Had a beginning: 'there was when he was not';
- Cannot comprehend the infinite God; and
- Must be liable to change.

Yet the Christ of the Gospel narratives, with their genealogies and fulfilment of prophecies, together with the New Testament epistles reveal the only Redeemer the world has been given. If Jesus Christ is rejected, God's publicized way of salvation through Him is rejected. Are you looking for the historical Jesus? The real Jesus? What is written in the Scriptures allows us to believe (John 20:30–31). It is by preaching the glory, grace, death, resurrection and ascension (and session) of the historical Jesus that the truth that Jesus Christ alone is 'the way, the truth and the life' and that no one can come to God except through Him (14:6) can be believed. This seemingly outrageous declaration was reinforced by the Apostle Paul in his First Epistle to the Corinthians: 'I declare to you the gospel . . . by which also you are saved . . . that Christ died for our sins according to the Scriptures, and that He was buried, and that He rose again the third day according to the Scriptures' (1 Cor. 15:1–4). Sadly, Islam rejects Him and thus it rejects God's free offer of salvation.

NOTES

1 From Hamadi Al-Aslani's tract 'Islamic View of Jesus' (details unknown). The Maulana Wahiduddin Khan translation of the Quran says, 'We are God's helpers, we believe in God. Bear witness that we have surrendered ourselves' (Sura 3:52), indicating again that Islam wants to contradict the New Testament's witness to Jesus Christ's person and glory.

2 The number eight in the Bible represents 'new beginnings'. Jesus met with His disciples and doubting Thomas the Sunday *after* His resurrection a week earlier. This was the start of the Lord's Day-Sabbath for Christians. See my book *The Real Lord's Prayer* (Leominster: Day One, 2012), pp. 100–109.

3 It is important to grasp that 'the rock' is *not* Peter (whose name means a 'stone', *petros*) but the enlightened testimony of Peter which confessed Jesus to be 'the Christ, the Son of the living God'.

4 See Appendix 2 for a full list of names and titles given to Jesus Christ the Messiah in the Scriptures.

5 Even the Old Covenant under Moses required faith in a forgiving God (Ps. 4:1a; 32:1–2; 130:3–4; Hab. 2:4; Rom. 3:30–31; 4:3).

6 See also Matt. 20:16; 22:14; 1 Cor. 1:26–31; Eph. 1:4; James 2:5; 1 Peter 2:4, 9.

7 See William Hendriksen, *The Gospel of John* (London: Banner of Truth Trust, 1969), p. 71.

8 Herveus, quoted in P. E. Hughes, *A Commentary on the Epistle to the Hebrews* (Grand Rapids, MI: Eerdmans, 1977), p. 60.

9 T. C. Hammond, *In Understanding Be Men* (London: IVP, 1971), p. 101.

The divinity of Christ

Christ Jesus, . . . being in the form of God, did not consider it robbery to be equal with God. (Phil. 2:6)

Islam says that Christ was one of the foremost prophets who brought truth to His age. He is to be honoured. He was sinless, but He was a lesser prophet than Muhammad and was definitely not God in human flesh. Islam also teaches that Jesus did not die on the cross (Sura 4:157), and many Muslims claim that Judas was crucified in His place.[1] As this latter issue is not historically clear, Muslims sometimes say that Jesus only swooned on the cross, with some (only the Ahmadiyya sect) claiming that after He recovered He travelled to India, married and died. By denying Jesus' deity Islam rejects the coming of God's only begotten Son in the flesh. However, the New Testament says, 'Who is a liar but he who denies that Jesus is the Christ? He is the antichrist who denies the Father and the Son' (1 John 2:22).

The Son of God is revealed in the Bible as the Word (*logos*) who became flesh (John 1:1). His deity was not abandoned, reduced or contracted; nor did He cease to exercise the divine function which was His before His incarnation. The incarnation was not a diminishing of His deity but an acquiring of humanity. Thus Jesus Christ was not half God and half man but 100 per cent man and 100 per cent God. The Westminster Shorter Catechism question 21 asks, 'Who is the Redeemer of God's elect?' The answer is: 'The Lord Jesus Christ, who, being the eternal Son of God, became man, and so was, and continueth to be, God and man in two distinct natures, and one person, for ever.'

Early Christian thought

The early church followed the Jews in a belief in monotheism (1 Cor. 8:4,

6; 1 Tim. 2:5), but they proclaimed Christ to be divine (John 1:1). Ignatius (AD 50–115) spoke of the distinction between the three Person. Theophilus of Antioch (*c.*186) was the first to speak of a 'triad' in God. Athenagoras (*c.*178) spoke of God in three Persons. Tertullian of Carthage (160–240), however, was left to express it fully and he developed the doctrine of the Trinity building on the labours of his predecessors. He asserted a real distinction of Persons which belonged to the substance of the divine essence. To him 'belongs the distinction of first using the words "Person", "Substance" [and] "Trinity" as applied to the Godhead'.[2] His ideas have been retained to this day. Origen (184–254) asserted the eternal generation of the Son and taught that 'the Trinity was a living Fellowship of Persons. In that living process the Son is eternally generated by the Father, and the Spirit eternally proceeds from the Father and the Son.'[3] The doctrine of the Trinity that was affirmed at the Council of Nicaea in AD 325 was that substantially formulated by Tertullian and Origen. Athanasius, Augustine and John Calvin also all had a great contribution to make in formulating this doctrine.

The Bible points to the unity of Jesus' person:

It is always the same Person who speaks, whether the consciousness that finds utterance be human or divine (John 10:30; 17:5; cf. Matt. 27:46; John 19:28) . . . Human attributes and actions are sometimes ascribed to the Person designated by a divine title (Acts 20:28; 1 Cor. 2:8; Col. 1:13, 14). On the other hand, divine attributes and actions are ascribed to the Person designated by a human title (John 3:13; 6:62; Rom. 9:5).[4]

He had perfect humanity and did not sin, nor could He sin—He was impeccable (John 8:46; 2 Cor. 5:21; Heb. 4:15; 9:14; 1 Peter 2:22; 1 John 3:5).[5] His humanity was important in order for Him to be our atoning substitute: to suffer and die. The perfection of His humanity was important as only a sinless man could make successful atonement for others. His divinity was important as it was only as God that His sacrifice could have infinite value and bear the full wrath of God (Ps. 40:7–10; 130:3). Jesus Christ is not man deified or God humanized; He was indivisibly one Christ and indissolubly divine and human. He never ceased to be the eternal God.

His offices[6]

The Bible ascribes to the Messiah a *three-fold office*, that is, He has three functions or duties, all of which are required of Him in His work as Messiah. These are:

- Prophet and Teacher (Luke 24:19)
- Priest and Saviour (Heb. 2:17)
- King and Ruler (Rev. 19:16)

Martin Luther was probably the first to teach explicitly that Christ was Prophet, Priest and King, and John Calvin is the man who has the distinction of developing it fully in his *Institutes of the Christian Religion*: 'That faith may find in Christ a solid ground of salvation and so rest in Him, we must set out with this principle that the office which He received from the Father consists of three parts. For He was appointed Prophet, King and Priest.'[7] From that time until now, Protestant writers have spoken of this three-fold office and it was embraced by the Westminster Confession (1647) and the Shorter Catechism (questions 24–26), the London Baptist Confession of 1689 and the Independent Savoy Declaration of 1658.

PROPHET AND TEACHER

'Christ executeth the office of a prophet, in revealing to us, by His Word and Spirit, the will of God for our salvation' (Shorter Catechism Q. 24). A prophet 'is one who speaks for another' and 'one who speaks to man for God'. He 'is one who receives divine revelation and passes it on'. He foretells the future—prophecy. He also forthtells, as his task is to impart and interpret the moral and spiritual aspects of the law through preaching. This gift of foretelling was from Christ (1 Peter 1:11). The Old Testament predicted that the Messiah would have this office (Deut. 18:15; cf. Acts 3:22–23; Isa. 60:1–2). In the New Testament, Jesus Christ speaks of Himself as a prophet (Matt. 24:3–35; Luke 13:33; John 12:49–50) and His contemporaries accepted Him as such (Matt. 21:11; Luke 24:19; John 7:40). It was the Saviour's task, while on earth, to communicate divine knowledge to the people of God. He still functions as a prophet while in His heavenly session (John 14:26; 16:12–14; Rom. 8:34; Heb. 1:1–2). Men sent from God preaching scriptural faith and sincere repentance was a heavenly sign from God in Bible times, and is still today. God expects us to listen and respond to the gospel with faith and repentance (Eph. 4:21). From the first moment spiritual life begins until we are brought into fellowship with the Father by the work of redemption, Jesus Christ is our only Prophet and Teacher.

PRIEST AND SAVIOUR

'Christ executeth the office of a priest, in His once offering up of Himself a sacrifice to satisfy divine justice, and reconcile us to God; and in making continual intercession for us' (Shorter Catechism Q. 25). A priest is a mediator. He is one who stands between God and His worshippers. He is authorized to appear before God and to act on behalf of men. While a prophet comes down from God to man and represents God among men, a priest goes Godward from man and represents God before the people. The priest has the special privilege of approaching God and of acting on behalf of the people. The Old Testament prophesied of the coming Messiah's priesthood (Ps. 110:4; Zech. 6:13). In the New Testament, Jesus' priestly work is spoken of in Mark 10:45; 1 Corinthians 5:7; and 1 John 1:2. However, the Epistle to the Hebrews is the only place where Christ is called a 'priest' (Heb. 3:1; 4:14; 6:20; etc.). The priest is to bring a sacrifice for sin before God. At Calvary, Christ brought Himself as the 'sacrificial victim' and made satisfaction for our sins (Heb. 9:14). The priest intercedes for us, and as Mediator Christ prays for the church: this is part of His work and not a supplement to it (Rom. 8:34; Heb. 7:25). Jesus prayed for His people before they were saved (John 17:20).

- He is a real and perfect Priest (Heb. 7:24, 26).
- He is a living Priest (Heb. 7:25).
- He is the only Priest (Heb. 9:15).

A priest for ever

In Islam, 'to stress the superiority of Muhammad over Isa (Jesus Christ), several *hadith* claim that on the Day of Judgment Isa will point all those seeking his intercession for them to Muhammad, who alone will be able to intercede for his followers. Muhammad is thus established as far greater than Isa.'[8] This teaching is not found in the Quran but has authority for Muslims from the Hadith: 'Narrated Abu Huraira: " . . . So they will go to Isa and say, 'O Isa! You are Allah's Apostle and His Word which He sent to Mary, and a superior soul created by Him'"' (Al-Bukhari, 6:236).[9] This statement makes no sense to Christians because it was written at least three centuries *after* the Scriptures which teach that the crucified, buried, resurrected and ascended Jesus is 'a High Priest . . . fitting for us' and that we need no other to help us approach God Almighty: 'He is also able to save to the uttermost those who come to God through Him, since He always lives to make intercession for them. For such a High Priest was fitting for us' (Heb. 7:25–26).

Islam removes Jesus Christ and replaces Him with another messenger. In Islam it appears that the saviour and mediator between Allah and mankind is actually the Quran itself! Hence it is learnt by heart (i.e. in Arabic) from youth. Muhammad is only 'the Messenger'. Islam definitely removes Jesus and replaces Him with the Quran: there is no other mediator between Muslims and Allah. This, however, does not stop Muslims, when in trouble or pain, crying out to Muhammad for help!

This is encouraged by Muslim prayer itself, which concludes by addressing Muhammad directly as if he were alive. In a passage called 'Tashahhud' recited at the end of every Muslim prayer, Muhammad is directly spoken to: 'All compliments, prayers and pure words are due to Allah. *Peace be upon you, O Prophet, and the mercy of Allah and his blessings.*'[10]

Christ's session[11]

The Lord Jesus gives those who believe access to Himself and His priestly ministry. His priestly ministry belongs to the present as well as the past, for He is now ascended and in heavenly session He lives not only for His own glory but for our eternal salvation also. He lives in heaven for us, as John Owen says, 'to carry on the complete work of purchased grace' appearing in the presence of God for us in order to sanctify our present imperfect works.[12] If Christ Jesus had not ascended and entered into His session, His words to Peter, 'I have prayed for you', could not be applied to all God's adopted children; however, He sits at the right hand of God interceding to secure for us salvation's full and final adoption (Rom. 8:23). Christ our Saviour, having died for us, sprinkles us with His precious blood to cleanse us. The application of the blood to believers' hearts is by the Spirit (sent forth from the Father and the Son) at Christ's request (Heb. 9:14). As Ferguson says, 'Those who enjoy communion with Him are reassured there is no lack in them that He cannot meet, no emptiness He cannot fill, no sin He cannot forgive, no enemy that can withstand the fact that the Christ who died for them lives forever for them at God's right hand.'[13] The habitual grace given to believers post-conversion is to be recognized as being different from the indwelling of the Holy Spirit, being produced by His ministry to us. Thus we can say that because of our union to Christ he now adds 'grace to grace' in order that His people might persevere to the end of life. 'He pardons past sins and also sanctifies our present imperfect works.'[14]

KING AND RULER

'Christ executeth the office of a king, in subduing us to Himself, in ruling and defending us, and in restraining and conquering all His and our enemies' (Shorter Catechism Q. 26). As the Son, Christ naturally shares universal dominion (Col. 1:16). The Old Testament loves to speak of the Messiah's kingly role (Num. 24:17; Isa. 9:6; Dan. 7:13–14; Zech. 6:13). The New Testament also prophesies His future rule over an everlasting kingdom (Luke 1:31–33). As the Second Person of the Trinity, equal in power and glory with the eternal Father and possessing inherent sovereign dominion, He is Ruler over the whole universe (1 Cor. 15:25–27; Heb. 2:8). As Mediator the function of king is conferred upon Him by the authority of the Godhead as His reward (Eph. 1:20–23; Phil. 2:7–11). As the Son of Man, he sits upon the mediatorial throne in heaven (Heb. 1:3). His kingdom is spiritual, with spiritual influences and graces for believers (Luke 17:21). With a spiritual end in view the Word and Holy Spirit are its administration (Matt. 12:28; Rom 14:17). The present rule is invisible; however, His future rule will be visible and perfect (Luke 19:11–27; 2 Tim 4:18; 2 Peter 1:11).

The witness and testimony of the Christian Scriptures to the Lord Jesus Christ is clear and is there for all to believe. Islam attacks the uniqueness and divinity of our Saviour. Although saying that Jesus Christ is to be honoured, Islam rejects His atoning death on the cross, thinking that (perhaps) Judas was crucified in His place. But the doctrine of Jesus Christ is central to the Christian faith: 'Jesus Christ is the very centre of Christianity and the deity of Christ remains the citadel of its faith.'[15] For R. L. Dabney, it is its most distinctive testimony: 'This may be called a prime article of revealed theology.' What's more, 'If the apostles did not intend to teach this doctrine they have certainly had the remarkable ill luck of producing the very impression they sought to avoid.'[16]

THE DOCTRINE PROVED

- Jesus Himself had the sense that He was the Son of God in a unique way (Luke 2:9; John 5:24–26; 7:29; 10:36; 11:25).

- The Bible ascribes divine attributes to Christ (Isa. 9:6; [10:21]; Micah 5:2; John 21:17; Heb. 1:11–12; Rev. 1:8, 17).

- The Bible ascribes divine works to Christ (Mark 2:5–7; Col. 1:16–17; Heb. 1:1–3).

- The Bible ascribes divine honour to Christ (Matt. 28:19; John 5:19–29; John 14:1; 2 Cor. 13:14; Heb. 1:6).

- The three Persons of the Godhead work side-by-side in the Bible (Gen. 1:26; Matt. 28:19; Luke 3:22; John 14:16, 23; 2 Cor. 13:14; Gal. 4:6).

- Other NT verses for consideration: John 1:1; Acts 20:28; Rom. 9:5; Phil. 2:6; Col. 2:2; 1 Tim. 3:16; Heb. 1:8; 1 John 5:20; Rev. 1:8–18.

NOTES

1 Note that Sura 4:157–158 states that Jesus was not crucified. The discredited and false *Gospel of Barnabas* claims that Judas was crucified instead (ch. 216–217); also see Abdullah Kareem, 'The Crucifixion of Judas', http://www.answering-christianity.com/abdullah_smith/crucifixion_of_judas.htm. A more reasoned Muslim article, giving other options, is 'Who Died on the Cross?', Crescent Project, https://www.crescentproject.org/articles-blog/2017/3/24/who-died-on-the-cross.

2 R. A. Finlayson, *The Story of Theology* (London: Tyndale Press, 1969), pp. 16–17. I am indebted to this work for some of what follows.

3 Ibid., p. 17.

4 Louis Berkhof, 'The Natures of Christ', in *Manual of Christian Doctrine* (2nd edn; Arlington Heights, IL: Christian Liberty Press, 2003), p. 73.

5 See my book *The Real Lord's Prayer* (Leominster: Day One, 2012), pp. 73–78.

6 For what follows I am grateful to A. A. Hodge, *Evangelical Theology* (Edinburgh: Banner of Truth Trust, 1976), p. 185; and T. C. Hammond, *In Understanding Be Men* (London: IVP, 1971), pp. 103f.

7 J. Calvin, *Institutes of the Christian Religion* (Grand Rapids, MI: Associated Publishers and Authors Inc., [n. d.]), 2.15.1.

8 Patrick Sookhdeo, *Is the Muslim Isa the Biblical Jesus?* (McLean, VA: Isaac Publishing, 2012),

pp. 13–14. 'The origin of the name "Isa" is obscure. It was invented by Muhammad . . . [it] was formed by inverting the order of the Hebrew letters that make up the name Yesu'a (= Joshua = Jesus) . . . [it] has no connection with the Biblical and historical figure of Jesus of Nazareth.' Ibid., p. 11.

9 Ibid., pp. 14–15.

10 The emphasis is mine.

11 Based on my book *Getting to Grips with Prayer: Its Realities, Challenges and Potential* (Leominster: Day One, 2017), p. 34.

12 Sinclair Ferguson, *The Trinitarian Devotion of John Owen* (Sanford, FL: Reformation Trust Publishing, 2014), p. 83.

13 Ibid., p. 86.

14 Ibid., p. 93.

15 Finlayson, *Story of Theology*, p. 7.

16 R. L. Dabney, *Systematic Theology* (Edinburgh: Banner of Truth Trust, 1996), p. 183.

Abraham, friend of God

Abraham believed God, and it was accounted to him for righteousness. (Rom. 4:3)

Abraham (Ibrahim in Islam) is viewed by Muslims as an example of a believer in Allah *par excellence* and a 'friend' of God (Suras 16:120–121; 4:125). The Quran speaks of him as the founder of true religion (revived by Muhammad and his followers; Suras 2:130–140; 3:65–68; 16:120–124) but has little to say about his life and concentrates on his conflict with his people's polytheism.[1] Abraham holds a special place in Islam as the champion of monotheism (Sura 6:75–80). He is claimed by Muslims to be their prophet alone: 'Abraham was neither a Jew nor a Christian. He was . . . one who surrendered himself to God' (Sura 3:67). This stands in sharp contrast with the New Testament's view of Abraham. The Lord Jesus Christ spoke well of him and holds Abraham up as a worthy example of a man of faith and of God (Matt. 8:11; Luke 16:29; etc.). The Apostle Paul held Abraham in high esteem too. 'For the promise that he would be the heir of the world was not to Abraham or to his seed through the law, but through the righteousness of faith' (Rom. 4:13).

The Quran mentions the 'Scriptures of Abraham' (Sura 87:18–19) which are purported to be revelations given to Abraham.[2] The Quranic version of the 'sacrifice' of Isaac by Abraham differs greatly from the Old Testament account (Gen. 22:2, 9–14). The Quran (Sura 37:99–107) speaks of a similar type of event but no name is mentioned in the text; however, most Muslims believe that Ishmael was present.[3] Muslims believe that Abraham and Ishmael were the founders of the Ka'bah (in Mecca, Saudi Arabia), the holiest shrine in Islam (Sura 2:124–127) after Abraham rid it of idols. No such event is recorded in the Bible. Gerald Hawting's comment is pertinent:

Islam sought to establish its independence against other forms of monotheism and to assert its identity as the only legitimate representative of Abraham's religion. It seems likely, therefore, that the idea of Abraham as the builder of the Ka'ba originated in connection with the claim that he was the forefather of the religion that had the Ka'ba as its central shrine, Islam.[4]

Islam redefines the faith that made Abraham right with God by attempting to 'rewrite' Genesis and other Old Testament texts.[5] The biblical evidence for the type of faith that made Abraham right with God and gave him the universal reputation as the 'friend of God' is ignored by Islam (2 Chr. 20:7; Isa. 41:8; Acts 7:7–32). Various myths are given credence in the Quran, making Abraham's birth similar to that of Jesus, and Abraham is recorded as surviving the fiery furnace (Sura 21:68–69), which echoes the experience of the three Hebrews, Shadrach, Meshach and Abed-Nego (Dan. 3:23).[6]

Extra-biblical traditions

Abraham is held in high esteem in Judaism also.[7] The second-century book of Jubilees says that 'Abraham was perfect in all his deeds with the Lord, and well pleasing in righteousness all the days of his life' (23:10).[8] The Jews of Paul's day considered Abraham to have been the only righteous man of his generation and the rabbis said that Abraham had a thorough knowledge of the law and obeyed it in all its details. A Jewish contemporary prayer reveals this attitude: 'Therefore you, O Lord, God of the righteous, have not appointed repentance for the righteous, for Abraham and Isaac and Jacob, who did not sin against you, but you have appointed repentance for me, who am a sinner.'[9] 'Talmudic and midrashic writings recall that in his battle against eastern kings, Abraham threw dust which turned into swords, and chaff which turned into arrows.'[10] 'Later Jewish traditions make him also the conqueror of Damascus; while others . . . [have him] preaching to the idolatrous

Babylonians and Egyptians the one true God. Abraham is far more than a historical figure; he is the embodiment of those exalted ideals which made the Israelites what they were.'[11]

However, Abraham was *not* perfect as the Jewish book of Jubilees claims; we know Abraham was a sinner because his sins are recorded for us in the book of Genesis (Gen. 20:2; Ps. 14:1–3). In the light of the pre-Islamic Jewish Midrash, was Muhammad misled about Abraham's holiness and righteousness?[12]

The religion of Abraham

Abraham appears in the Bible first in Genesis 11:26 as Abram son of Terah.[13] In spite of his background Abraham believed in the one true Jehovah (God) (Gen. 12:1–4). Abraham is mentioned by name around 240 times in the Bible and is a hero of faith in Hebrews 11. He is also mentioned in Paul's Epistle to the Romans and in Galatians, where he is an example (along with King David) of a person who has true saving faith. In Genesis 25 we read of his death and burial by Isaac and Ishmael in the cave of Machpelah, where his wife Sarah's remains had been laid (vv. 8–10). Genesis 12–25 describes his life after leaving Ur of the Chaldeans for Canaan, showing clearly that his reputation was rooted in a historical person.

The Old Testament Abraham is the best and clearest example of God's dealings with men and women in the past dispensation and now in the new. In Romans 4 we have a powerful defence of the proposition that justification before God Almighty is by faith alone. There Paul presents Abraham's salvation as an example of how God deals with men in all ages and at all times and from all people groups. This respected and revered man of faith who is the father of the Jews is an example of the way God saves sinners:

What then shall we say that Abraham our father has found according to the flesh? For if Abraham was justified by works, he has something to boast about, but not before God. For what does the Scripture say? 'Abraham believed God, and it was accounted to him for righteousness.' Now to him who works, the wages are not counted as grace but as debt. (Rom. 4:1–4)

Abraham was not as 'saintly' as Jewish and Islamic tradition makes him out to be, and it is unscriptural to deny him the failings of a fallen nature as a child of Adam (Rom. 3:23; 5:12ff.). The Bible in our hands is the antidote to apocryphal and heretical teaching.[14] There is a tendency for every one of us to fall back on our own works for salvation, especially if we either are ignorant of the teaching of Scripture or deny its implications. Sadly, salvation by works is what Islam seems to teach (Sura 4:124–125). To feel it necessary to do something to atone for our sins and therefore to appease the wrath of God is a big mistake.

Jesus spoke against this self-righteous attitude when He corrected the Jewish scribes about their error regarding life after death:

Jesus answered and said to them, 'You are mistaken, not knowing the Scriptures nor the power of God. For in the resurrection they neither marry nor are given in marriage, but are like angels of God in heaven. But concerning the resurrection of the dead, have you not read what was spoken to you by God, saying, "I am the God of Abraham, the God of Isaac, and the God of Jacob"? God is not the God of the dead, but of the living.' (Matt. 22:29–32)

We see from this that it is possible to read and even study the Scriptures and not understand them unless we are given light by the Holy Spirit of God (1 Cor. 2:12–14). Abraham was a believer and his faith justified him in God's sight. This is what the Old Testament reveals to us: 'he believed in the LORD, and He accounted it to him for righteousness' (Gen. 15:6). This is Abraham's true reputation stripped of false news, exaggerated honour and the wrong theology that asks men to do what their fallen sinful natures cannot do: 'As it is written: "There is none righteous, no, not one; there is none who understands; there is none who seeks after God"' (Rom. 3:10–11).

Abraham's peace

We have seen that Paul went back to the Old Testament Scriptures to find out what God said and did. There he saw how the Scriptures reveal the way of salvation for *then* and *now*, that is, for the Old Testament dispensation and the New. In Romans 4:3, 7–8 Paul quotes from Genesis 15:6 and Psalm 32:1–2 to prove that the Old Testament taught that the imputed righteousness of God unto justification was the gospel:

[Abraham] believed in the LORD, and He accounted it to him for righteousness. (Gen. 15:6)

Blessed is he whose transgression is forgiven,
Whose sin is covered.
Blessed is the man to whom the LORD does not impute iniquity. (Ps. 32:1–2)

The words 'accounted' and 'impute' in Hebrew mean that something is placed to one's account. Paul uses parallel Greek words to press home this doctrine of justification by faith alone and to emphasize its importance (Rom. 4:1–4). We are told clearly in Romans 4:2 that Abraham was not accepted by God because of his goodness or good deeds: 'if Abraham was justified by works, he has something to boast about, but not before God.' How, then, was he accepted as a 'friend of God' and saved? This is explained by the words Paul quotes from Genesis 15 and Psalm 32, repeating them in Romans 4 eight times in eleven verses and eleven times in the whole of the chapter. When it comes to God's way of salvation which flows from the free grace of God to unmerited sinners, the imputation of righteousness is key. This doctrine has become known to us, since the Reformation, as the doctrine of justification by faith alone. Martin Luther rediscovered it in the sixteenth century while studying the book of Psalms and the Epistles to the Romans and Galatians independent of Roman Catholic dogma which added good works to faith both to justify and to sanctify the sinner. Luther preached that justification by faith alone is the article by which the church stands or falls. This is a key doctrine of the Christian faith, and the preaching of imputed righteousness has been central in every revival of the church. Paul emphasizes that this was the way of salvation from the beginning of time. He could have written about Jeremiah's words in Jeremiah 23:5–7:

'Behold, the days are coming,' says the LORD,
'That I will raise to David a Branch of righteousness;
A King shall reign and prosper,
And execute judgment and righteousness in the earth.
In His days Judah will be saved,
And Israel will dwell safely;
Now this is His name by which He will be called:
    THE LORD OUR RIGHTEOUSNESS.'

Or he could have referred to Habakkuk 2:4: 'Behold the proud, his soul is not upright in him; but the just shall live by his faith.' Christians believe that the Holy Spirit led the prophet Habakkuk to speak about Abraham and King David and all who would be accounted righteous by faith alone (Rom. 3:26). Writing on Romans 3:26, 'just and the justifier of the one who has faith in Jesus', Charles H. Spurgeon said,

Being justified by faith, we have peace with God. Conscience accuses no longer. Judgment now decides for the sinner instead of against him. Memory looks back upon past sins, with deep sorrow for the sin, but yet with no dread of any penalty to come; for Christ has paid the debt of His people to the last jot and tittle, and received the divine receipt; and unless God can be so unjust as to demand double payment for one debt, no soul for whom Jesus died as a substitute can ever be cast into hell. It seems to be one of the very principles of our enlightened nature to believe that God is just; we feel that it must be so, and this gives us our terror at first; but is it not marvelous that this very same belief that God is just, becomes afterwards the pillar of our confidence and peace![15]

God's covenant with Abraham was on the basis of faith alone (Rom. 4:13). However, Islam redefines the faith that made Abraham right with God by attempting to rewrite and re-interpret Genesis and other Old Testament texts, as seen above.[16] Muslims insist that the Hebrew Masoretic text has been tampered with and they feel free to claim that their own divine narrative, the Quran, was given to Muhammad by the archangel Gabriel. Islam therefore claims that 'The Jews and the Christians have been editing their "Book of God" from its very inception.'[17] Many Muslims are willing to debate with Christians using spurious reasoning and slanderous innuendo against the Scriptures of Christianity, claiming that 'the "Holy Bible" contains a motley type of literature, which [consists of] the embarrassing kind, the sordid, and the obscene—all under the same cover—a Christian is forced to concede equal spiritual import and authority to all'.[18] If this statement was made about the Quran, its author would be regarded as worthy of death under Islamic sharia law! What Islam grants for itself, it denies to others. However, we know that the children of the flesh are persecutors of the true seed of God; as Paul indicated, 'as he who was born according to the flesh then persecuted him who was born according to the Spirit, even so it is now' (Gal. 4:29).

NOTES

1 Christine Schirrmacher, *The Islamic View of Major Christian Teachings* (Bonn: Culture and Science, 2008), p. 66.

2 S. B. Noegel and B. N. Wheeler (eds.), *Historical Dictionary of Prophets in Islam and Judaism* (Lanham, MD: Scarecrow Press, 2010), p. 8.

3 'Older Koran commentaries, however, come to different conclusions.' Schirrmacher, *Islamic View*, p. 68.

4 Gerald Hawting, 'The Religion of Abraham and Islam', in M. Goodman, G. H. van Kooten and J. van Ruiten (eds.), *Abraham, the Nations, and the Hagarites* (Leiden: Brill, 2010), p. 498.

5 See Maulana Wahiduddin Khan, *The Quran: A New Translation*, ed. Farida Khanam (New Delhi: Goodword Books, 2009), p.164.

6 Noegel and Wheeler, *Historical Dictionary*, p. 6.

7 The name Abraham means 'Father of a multitude of nations'.

8 The book of Jubilees was originally written in Hebrew.

9 'Prayer of Manasseh 8', Biblia.com, https://biblia.com/bible/prMan8.

10 Noegel and Wheeler, *Historical Dictionary*, p. 7.

11 Hastings, *Greater Men and Women of the Bible*, Vol. 1, pp. 112–113.

12 Hawting, 'Religion of Abraham and Islam', p. 482.

13 Sura 6:74 has Abraham's father as Azar and not Terah. See also Luke 3:34.

14 Christians today are to be like the great Reformer Martin Luther in this regard: he challenged the errors of the Roman Catholic Church of his day because he read the Bible for himself and believed its witness to be true.

15 C. H. Spurgeon, *Morning and Evening*, 25 September, Morning (McLean, VA: MacDonald, [n.d.]).

16 Khan, *The Quran*, p.164.

17 Islam claims that the Quran has been protected by God from error or change. See Ahmed Deedat, *Is the Bible God's Word?* (Durban: Islamic Propagation Centre International, 1989), pp. 7, 21.

18 Ibid., p. 6.

A prophet like Moses[1]

He [Jesus] was transfigured before them. His face shone like the sun, and His clothes became as white as the light. And behold, Moses and Elijah appeared to them, talking with Him. (Matt. 17:2–3)

Jesus' office as Prophet was first described by Moses in Deuteronomy 18:15–19, when he spoke about the Messiah yet to come:

The LORD said to me: '. . . I will raise up for them a Prophet like you from among their brethren, and will put My words in His mouth, and He shall speak to them all that I command Him. And it shall be that whoever will not hear My words, which He speaks in My name, I will require it of him.' (Deut. 18:17–19)

However, Islam claims that Muhammad is the prophet foretold in these verses. Some Muslims argue tenaciously that because Jesus' name is not given in the text of Deuteronomy 18, and because the prophet is to be 'like Moses', who did not die for the sins of Israel or rise again on the third day, this prophecy cannot be speaking about Jesus Christ but must rather point to another prophet.[2] Muslim apologists have produced lists of criteria pertaining to Moses and Muhammad saying that both were married and had children, and both were leaders and led battles. Muslims also make the following assertions to confuse untaught Christians and take their minds away from the truth as it is in Jesus:

- Jesus had a miraculous birth; Moses did not.
- Jesus was rejected by the Jews; Moses was not.
- Jesus was crucified; Moses was not.
- Moses brought God's laws to his people as Muhammad did.

What they fail to make clear is that any prophet could claim for himself many parallels with Moses.

How do we answer Muslims regarding these wild assertions? What do the Scriptures say? In what way does Deuteronomy 18 speak about Jesus Christ?

Firstly, we can show that:

- Jesus as a baby was saved by God from death (Matt. 2:16), as was Moses (Exod. 1:17; 2:2–10).
- Jesus performed miracles (Matt. 14:13–21; Luke 7:11–17), as did Moses in Egypt (Exod. 7:10, 19ff.).
- Jesus was descended from Jacob (Matt. 1:2, 16; Luke 3:23, 34), as was Moses (Exod. 2:1; 3:15).
- Jesus was especially chosen by God, as was Moses (both their early lives are recorded in the Bible, but Muhammad is not given this honour or even named).
- Jesus the Messiah was sent to the elect Israel as God's chosen leader, as was Moses.
- Jesus was the architect of redemption and deliverance from bondage, as was Moses, who planned the Passover meal as well as the exodus from Egypt.
- Jesus is the Good Shepherd who gave His life for the sheep; Moses was a shepherd in Midian for forty years.
- Jesus gave God's words to the apostles (John 17:8); Moses gave God's laws to Israel (Exod. 20).

The New Testament states that Jesus was the one spoken of in Deuteronomy 18:

We have found Him of whom Moses in the law, and also the prophets, wrote. (John 1:45)

If you believed Moses, you would believe Me; for he wrote about Me. (John 5:46)

This is truly the Prophet who is to come into the world. (John 6:14)

For Moses truly said to the fathers, 'The LORD your God will raise up for you a Prophet like me from your brethren. Him you shall hear in all things, whatever He says to you. And it shall be that every soul who will not hear that Prophet shall be utterly destroyed from among the people' (Acts 3:22–23)

What is extraordinary about the Muslim claim that Deuteronomy 18 is about Muhammad is that Sura 3:50 quotes Jesus talking to his disciples and saying, 'I come to fulfil [the prediction] of the Torah which preceded me'! This agrees with the four New Testament texts quoted above.

Secondly, the Muslim claim that Muhammad is the prophet spoken of in Deuteronomy really rests on Muslims proving that Ishmael, from whom Arabs claim their ancestry, was a Jew! Deuteronomy 18:18 says, 'I will raise up for them a Prophet *like you from among their brethren*' (emphasis added). For the prophet of Islam to be the one foretold here, he would need to be a Jew, but Muhammad was an Arab. Both the Old and New Testaments make it clear that the Messiah and the Prophet to whom Moses referred would be:

- *From the family of Jacob, the elect grandson of Abraham, and not from his son Ishmael:* 'I see Him, but not now; I behold Him, but not near; a Star shall come out of Jacob; a Scepter shall rise out of Israel' (Num. 24:17); 'For they are not all Israel who are of Israel, nor are they all children because they are the seed of Abraham; but, "In Isaac your seed shall be called"' (Rom. 9:6b–7; see also Gen. 21:12; Heb. 11:18); 'For it is written that Abraham had two sons: the one by a bondwoman, the other by a freewoman. But he who was of the bondwoman was born according to the flesh, and he of the freewoman through promise . . . Now we, brethren, as Isaac was, are children of promise. But, as he who was born according to the flesh then persecuted him who was born according to the Spirit, even so it is now' (Gal. 4:22–23, 28–29).
- *From the house of King David:* 'And I will pour on the house of

David and on the inhabitants of Jerusalem the Spirit of grace and supplication; then they will look on Me whom they pierced. Yes, they will mourn for Him as one mourns for his only son, and grieve for Him as one grieves for a firstborn' (Zech. 12:10); 'I, Jesus, have sent My angel to testify to you these things in the churches. I am the Root and the Offspring of David, the Bright and Morning Star' (Rev. 22:16).

- *Born in Bethlehem:* 'But you, Bethlehem Ephrathah, though you are little among the thousands of Judah, yet out of you shall come forth to Me the One to be Ruler in Israel, whose goings forth are from of old, from everlasting' (Micah 5:2); 'Now after Jesus was born in Bethlehem of Judea in the days of Herod the king, behold, wise men from the East came to Jerusalem, saying, "Where is He who has been born King of the Jews? For we have seen His star in the East and have come to worship Him"' (Matt. 2:1–2).
- *God's Son:* 'For unto us a Child is born, unto us a Son is given, and the government will be upon His shoulder, and His name will be called Wonderful, Counselor, Mighty God [*El Gibor*], Everlasting Father, Prince of Peace' (Isa. 9:6; compare 10:20–21: 'And it shall come to pass in that day that the remnant of Israel . . . will return, the remnant of Jacob, to the Mighty God [*El Gibor*]'); '"Behold, the days are coming,' says the LORD, "that I will raise to David a Branch of righteousness; a King shall reign and prosper, and execute judgment and righteousness in the earth. In His days Judah will be saved, and Israel will dwell safely; now this is His name by which He will be called: THE LORD OUR RIGHTEOUSNESS [*Yahweh Tsidkenu*]"' (Jer. 23:5–6).

Although Muslims believe Sura 61:6 to be a prophecy from Jesus about 'Ahmad' (reckoned to be Muhammad) who would follow Him, we see from the above that Muhammad was not born in the prophetic line of Moses. 'Furthermore, internally, the Quran claims (Sura 29:27) that the priesthood belongs solely to the line of Isaac and Jacob, to which Muhammad had no part.'[3]

Thirdly, the Epistle to the Hebrews was written to prove the exclusive greatness of Jesus Christ; He is therein revealed to be the rightful heir to the title Messiah, the One who is greater than Moses:

Christ Jesus . . . was faithful to Him who appointed Him, as Moses also was faithful in all His house. For this One has been counted worthy of more glory than Moses . . . And Moses indeed was faithful in all His house as a servant . . . but Christ as a Son over His own house, whose house we are if we hold fast the confidence and the rejoicing of the hope firm to the end. (Heb. 3:1b–3, 5–6)

Fourthly, Jesus spoke of Moses as a witness to Himself in different places:

Then He said to them, O foolish ones, and slow of heart to believe in all that the prophets have spoken! Ought not the Christ to have suffered these things and to enter into His glory? And beginning at Moses and all the Prophets, He expounded to them in all the Scriptures the things concerning Himself. (Luke 24:25–27)

He said to them, 'Why are you troubled? And why do doubts arise in your hearts? Behold My hands and My feet, that it is I Myself. Handle Me and see, for a spirit does not have flesh and bones as you see I have.' . . . Then He said to them, 'These are the words which I spoke to you while I was still with you, that all things must be fulfilled which were written in the Law of Moses and the Prophets and the Psalms concerning Me.' And He opened their understanding, that they might comprehend the Scriptures. Then He said to them, 'Thus it is written, and thus it was necessary for the Christ to suffer and to rise from the dead the third day.' (Luke 24:38–39, 44–46)

Prophet of the covenant

Moses, through whom the covenant was given, and Elijah, through whom the covenant was restored, were seen with Jesus on the Mount of Transfiguration: 'He [Jesus] was transfigured . . . And behold, Moses and Elijah appeared to them, talking with Him' (Matt. 17:2–3).

This speaks loudly of Jesus Christ as God's Lawgiver and Prophet. Like Moses who pleaded with intense agony of soul for Israel when they sinned (Exod. 33:1–34:9) and like Elijah who was aware of Israel's apostasy and backsliding (Rom. 11:2–3), Jesus had been sent from heaven on the messianic mission to reclaim the kingdom of God. Christ's commission was sealed on the Mount by the voice of the Father and His brilliant presence: 'While he [Peter] was still speaking, behold, a bright cloud overshadowed them' (Matt. 17:5). This mode of divine revelation was reminiscent of the *Shekinah* Moses witnessed (the visible presence of God, Exod. 16:10; 40:34).

Jesus Christ was not one of a pantheon of prophets, He was the subject of their prophecies and their Lord. There were many anointed of God who spoke under inspiration in the Old Testament,[4] but Jesus was different, for He is the One of whom they spoke. He is worthy of their worship, service and love. There can be none greater than He:

God, who at various times and in various ways spoke in time past to the fathers by the prophets, has in these last days spoken to us by His Son, whom He has appointed heir of all things, through whom also He made the worlds; who being the brightness of His glory and the express image of His person, and upholding all things by the word of His power, when He had by Himself purged our sins, sat down at the right hand of the Majesty on high, having become so much better than the angels, as He has by inheritance obtained a more excellent name than they.

For to which of the angels did He ever say:

'You are My Son,

Today I have begotten you'?

And again:
'I will be to Him a Father,
And He shall be to Me a Son'? (Heb. 1:1–5)[5]

SON OF MAN

Jesus Christ took the Old Testament title of 'Son of Man' to Himself
(Matt. 24:27, 30; 25:13, 31; 26:64) as it pointed to His true humanity
manifested in the flesh, yet it has a clear messianic significance. He is '"a
man" but at the same time he is "*the* man". The title is linked in the book
of Daniel with the concept of everlasting rule and dominion (Dan. 7:14).
There He is the ultimate figure—both human and yet divine.'[6] Thus the
term 'Son of Man' is used by Jesus to denote His office as Messiah and
His work of redemption. John's vision on the Isle of Patmos proclaims
this: '[I saw] in the midst of the seven lampstands One like the Son of
Man, clothed with a garment down to the feet and girded about the chest
with a golden band' (Rev. 1:13).

WILLINGNESS TO BELIEVE?

Jesus said, 'For I have given to them the words which You have given Me;
and they have received them, and have known surely that I came forth
from You; and they have believed that You sent Me' (John 17:8). By these
'words' we understand the doctrines of the Christian faith. The disciples
believed that Jesus Christ was sent by God as the only Mediator between
God and man, and that He had given to them the words of eternal life.
Faith in Jesus Christ, as defined by the Bible, is not a step into the dark
but is 'knowledge passing into conviction and it is conviction passing
into confidence'.[7] With knowledge comes conviction and trust, which
motivates the will to believe.

Salvation is offered to all. Salvation is not restricted to white Anglo-
Saxons or to any other ethnicity. The teaching of Scripture is that

salvation is God's gift to all, irrespective of colour, nationality or birth creed. Jesus was born Jewish but His destiny as the Promised One (Isa. 53) was to save the world. Men have called Christianity 'the white man's religion', but they are wrong. They say this out of ignorance of God's plan to embrace all in Christ His Son. We are *all* called to believe and to repent: '[God] now commands all men everywhere to repent, because He has appointed a day on which He will judge the world in righteousness by the Man whom He has ordained. He has given assurance of this to all by raising Him from the dead' (Acts 17:30–31).

NOTES

1 See also my book *The Real Lord's Prayer: Christ's Glory and Grace in John 17* (Leominster: Day One, 2012), ch. 7. Help is also acknowledged from *Is There a Prediction of Muhammad in the Taurat?* (99 Truth Tracts, [n.d.]).

2 Ahmed Deedat, *What the Bible Says About Muhammad* (Birmingham: Islamic Propagation Centre International, 1989). See F. S. Copleston, *Christ or Mohammed?* (Harpenden: Islam's Challenge, 1989), pp. 147ff. for the strange claims made regarding Muhammad.

3 *Is There a Prediction of Muhammad in the Taurat?*

4 Former prophets: the Old Testament books of Joshua, Judges, Samuel and Kings. Latter prophets: the Old Testament books from Isaiah to Malachi, divided into the Major prophets and Minor prophets, the prophets to whom these books are ascribed. Major prophets: the prophets whose books come before that of Hosea, i.e. Isaiah, Jeremiah and Ezekiel, as opposed to the (twelve) Minor prophets, the prophets from Hosea to Malachi. *The Chambers Thesaurus*, 2004. © Chambers Harrap Publishers Ltd.

5 The NT is on this occasion quoting the OT from the prophetic Psalm 2 and 2 Sam. 7:14.

6 Allan Harman, *Daniel* (Darlington: Evangelical Press, 2007), p. 174.

7 John Murray, *Redemption: Accomplished and Applied* (London: Banner of Truth Trust, 1961), p. 111.

The resurrection

He is not here; for He is risen, as He said. (Matt. 28:6)

The Easter message is about life and not death. This means that everything depends on whether or not Jesus Christ rose from the dead. What are the facts about Easter?

1. Jews, Roman Catholics and Christians all agree that:
   • Jesus Christ was dead when taken from the cross.
   • He was buried in a new tomb.
   • On the third day His body was missing.
   • It was not removed by Jews or Romans, so where had it gone?

2. When the women arrived at the tomb early on Sunday morning (to continue the burial preparations on Jesus' body) they found the stone rolled away. They did not come to the wrong tomb: the Bible tells us that they took careful note of where it was and how to get back there (Matt. 27:61; Luke 23:53ff.; John 19:40–42).

3. On the same morning, the risen Saviour Jesus Christ appeared to His first witness Mary Magdalene (John 20:14, 18).

4. The Jewish and Roman officers could not find the missing body (Matt. 28:11–13).

5. The apostles and disciples of Jesus believed in His resurrection and were willing to die proclaiming it to be true and the fulfilment of Old Testament prophecy (Acts 2:30–35).

Islam and Sura 4

The resurrection of Jesus is not regarded as true by Islam, which claims that Jesus did not die on the cross and that Judas (or another) was substituted in His place. Muslims believe that there was no atoning death by Jesus of Nazareth, the Messiah of the Jews. Rather, the planned death of Jesus was thwarted when another person was crucified in His place: 'They did not kill him, nor did they crucify him, but it only seemed to them [as if it had been so]' (Sura 4:157). Muslims are therefore taught, in accordance with this sura, that whoever died on the cross (if it actually happened), it was *not* Jesus Christ: 'a substitute was made to look like Jesus and was crucified in his place while Jesus was taken straight up to heaven (without dying)'.[1] This idea has no historical substance or theological credibility. No secular historian doubts that Jesus was a historical person and that He was crucified and buried. So this assertion that it was not Jesus is without historical foundation. Some Muslims believe in the authority of a book called the *Gospel of Barnabas*, believing it to have been written by one of the disciples of Jesus. This book purports that it was Judas Iscariot who was crucified in the place of Jesus: 'The holy angels came and took Jesus out by the window that looketh toward the south. They bare him and placed him in the third heaven . . . Judas was so changed in speech and in face to be like Jesus that we believed him to be Jesus.'[2]

Because Islam believes that there was no death of Jesus at Calvary but instead transference into the 'third' heaven, there can be no bodily resurrection of Jesus in Islamic theology. This is contrary to the Scriptures. The Apostle Peter spoke about Jesus Christ's resurrection and its implications not only at Pentecost in Acts 2 but again to the 'Rulers of the people and the elders of Israel' in Acts 4:

Then Peter, filled with the Holy Spirit, said to them, ' . . . let it be known to you all, and to all the people of Israel, that . . . Jesus Christ of Nazareth, whom you crucified . . . God raised from the dead . . . This is the "stone which was rejected by you builders, which has become the chief cornerstone". Nor is there salvation in any other, for there is no other name under heaven given among men by which we must be saved.' (vv. 8a, 10–12)

The gospel and the resurrection

GOSPEL CONTENT

The Gospels give us the historical facts regarding Jesus' death and burial. He was laid in a new tomb, one owned by a rich man called Joseph of Arimathea, and there He lay until the third day when He rose from the dead. A Roman guard, with the agreement of Pontius Pilate and the Jewish hierarchy, was placed at His tomb so that the body would not be stolen by Jesus' followers (Matt. 27:62–66). The significance of Jesus' burial is three fold:

- It was the fulfilment of Old Testament prophecy: 'For you will not leave my soul in Sheol, nor will you allow Your Holy One to see corruption' (Ps. 16:10; John 19:37; Acts 2:29–32; 13:37).
- It proves that the Roman soldiers certified Jesus as dead when they took Him down from the cross. They were used to this procedure and were sure that He was truly deceased (Mark 15:43–45; John 19:38).
- Jesus' followers took careful note of the location of the new tomb where He was buried. This they revisited on the Sunday morning, but it was empty; thus they became eyewitnesses to Christ's resurrection (Mark 15:47).

THE THIRD DAY

The resurrection of Jesus Christ from the dead receives special attention in all four Gospels (Matt. 28; Mark 16; Luke 24; John 20). The women, who had accompanied Nicodemus when Jesus' body was bound in strips of linen with spices and laid in His new tomb, arrived early on Sunday morning to continue their burial preparations, expecting to find the corpse of Jesus in that sepulchre where they had laid it the night before. Instead, they found the stone rolled away and the tomb vacant (Luke 24:1–3). The Bible states that an angel of God had removed the stone

(Matt. 28:2). A short time later the risen Saviour appeared first to Mary Magdalene, then to the others. There were several resurrection appearances over a forty-day period, as noted in the New Testament, before Jesus Christ ascended into heaven to the Father (Acts 1:9).[3] This reminds us that the Christian faith is rooted in historical fact and is not human fiction.

THE TRIUMPH OF JESUS

Among the risen Saviour's last words before His ascension are those found at the end of the Gospel of Luke encouraging the Eleven to be His witnesses. It is clear from Luke 24:36–43 that the Eleven were finally convinced of His bodily resurrection when they heard His voice ('Why are you troubled? And why do doubts arise in your hearts?', v. 38), touched His hands ('Handle Me and see', v. 39) and observed Him eating ('a piece of a broiled fish and some honeycomb' at one sitting, v. 42).[4] Then He said to them,

'. . . all things must be fulfilled which were written in the Law of Moses and the Prophets and the Psalms concerning Me.' And He opened their understanding, that they might comprehend the Scriptures. Then He said to them, 'Thus it is written, and thus it was necessary for the Christ to suffer and to rise from the dead the third day.' (Luke 24:44–46)

Paul, in his First Epistle to the Corinthians (written *c.* AD 55), added more details about the events and people involved at the time of Christ's resurrection, ensuring that there can be no doubt about the content of the gospel message:

I declare to you the gospel which I preached to you, which also you received and in which you stand, by which also you are saved . . . For I delivered to you first of all that which I also received: that Christ died for our sins according to the Scriptures, and that

He was buried, and that He rose again the third day according to the Scriptures, and that He was seen by Cephas, then by the twelve. After that He was seen by over five hundred brethren at once, of whom the greater part remain to the present, but some have fallen asleep. After that He was seen by James, then by all the apostles. Then last of all He was seen by me also, as by one born out of due time. (1 Cor. 15:1–8)

Four things combine to make the gospel message we preach today faithful to the early church's beliefs:

- 'Christ died for our sins according to the Scriptures.' There is no ambiguity here: Jesus was crucified.
- 'He was buried': He was interred in a new tomb.
- 'He rose again the third day according to the Scriptures': the good news of Jesus Christ's bodily resurrection was believed and proclaimed.
- 'He was seen by Cephas, then by the twelve. After that He was seen by over five hundred brethren at once': there were contemporary eyewitnesses who were still alive at the time of Paul's writing.

The phrase 'according to the Scriptures' has reference to the Old Testament prophecies about the Messiah's death and the resurrection of the just (Job 14:14; 19:25–27; Ps. 16:10; 17:15; Isa. 26:19; Dan. 12:2; Hosea 13:14; Zech. 12:10; 13:6–7). Those who reject the truth of Christ's resurrection reject the testimony of the Holy Scriptures and charge its writers (the apostles and prophets) with fraud and deceit. One thing is clear, however: the Bible's writers never doubted the resurrection of God's Son from the dead. Islam's denial of the death, burial and third-day resurrection of Jesus Christ strikes at the very heart of the gospel and is aimed at the foundation of the church. This makes Islam and Christianity incompatible.

Chapter 11

The sign of Jonah[5]

Christians must therefore oppose all attempts to deny, invalidate or rewrite the resurrection accounts as found in the Gospels. Such attempts are on the increase, with more and more literature being produced from Islamic sources to discredit the historical accounts of the four Gospels.

One such effort is centred on the New Testament phrase 'the sign of the prophet Jonah'. The phrase is found in Matthew 12:40 and Luke 11:29 (cf. John 2:19) where it was used by our Lord during His teaching ministry with the apostles.

THE SIGN OF THE RESURRECTION

In his account Matthew makes it clear that the sign of Jonah was the resurrection of Christ from the dead:

But He answered and said to them, 'An evil and adulterous generation seeks after a sign, and no sign will be given to it except the sign of the prophet Jonah. For as Jonah was three days and three nights in the belly of the great fish, so will the Son of Man be three days and three nights in the heart of the earth.' (Matt 12:39–40)

Just as Jonah spent three days and three nights in the belly of the great fish, so Christ would be three days and three nights in the tomb and on the third day He would rise from the dead. The resurrection was thus the sign to the world that Jesus Christ is the Lord of glory, and the sign of Jonah was Christ's resurrection on the first day of the week. 'It follows that the sign of the new covenant should be the celebration and remembrance of the resurrection of Jesus Christ.'[6] The Christian Lord's Day (Rev. 1:10) is also a sign from God to an unbelieving world.

Similarly, the seventh-day Sabbath was given to the Jews as a sign that reminded them of their covenantal requirements: 'the children of Israel shall keep the Sabbath, to observe the Sabbath throughout their generations as a perpetual covenant. It is a sign between Me and the children of Israel forever; for in six days the LORD made the heavens and the earth, and on the seventh day He rested and was refreshed' (Exod. 31:16–17). It was a memorial to the covenant between God and Israel and it served as a weekly reminder of their special relationship with Him. God says of this sign, 'I . . . gave them My Sabbaths, to be a sign between them and Me' (Ezek. 20:12).

In John 2:18–22 the sign (of the temple) was a call to believe: 'So the Jews answered and said to Him, "What sign do You show to us, since You do these things?" Jesus answered and said to them, "Destroy this temple, and in three days I will raise it up"' (John 2:18–19). Jesus' words were again a reference to His resurrection. 'When He had risen from the dead, His disciples remembered that He had said this to them; and they believed the Scripture and the word which Jesus had said' (John 2:21).

MUSLIM CHALLENGES REGARDING THE 'SIGN OF JONAH'

The fact that 'the sign of Jonah' is repeated in the Gospels signifies its importance to the plan of redemption and the gospel message. It lays emphasis on the time when Christ was in the tomb before He rose bodily at His resurrection, and on the resurrection as a sign that tells the world that Jesus Christ is Lord. Islam refuses to accept that Jesus was in the tomb for three day and nights and endeavours to interpret the biblical texts concerning the sign in a way that contradicts the New Testament's testimony. One Islamic writer asks,

A fish swallows Jonah. Was he dead or alive when swallowed? . . . Surely dead men don't cry and don't pray! . . . Was he dead or alive for three days and nights? Alive! Alive! Alive! is the unanimous answer from the Jew, the Christian and the Muslim! If Jonah was alive for three days and three nights, then Jesus also ought to have been . . . Jesus is *supposed* to be in the tomb on the night of Friday . . . You will no doubt note that the *grand total* is *one* day and *two* nights, and *not* three days and three nights . . . is this not the mightiest hoax in history?[7]

Challenging the resurrection using the phrase 'the sign of the prophet Jonah' and ignoring the obvious meaning of the New Testament accounts is unbelieving mischief. How should Christians reply to such attacks?

We need to think about the Jewish use of time. If Jesus was actually in the new tomb for only one day and two nights (from Friday evening until Sunday morning), how do we explain the statement 'three days and three nights'? Three things are pertinent:

- In first-century Palestine, when counting a time period, the Jews took any part of the day to mean the whole day. For example, Jesus' first appearance to the apostles and the women on resurrection day (Sunday) was followed by a second appearance 'after eight days' (John 20:19, 26). This, in Jewish parlance, meant one week later (what we would count as seven days later).

- '[St] Augustine of Hippo finds this particular sign instructive and clarifying for understanding the nature of signs. Augustine reads the sign of Jonah as a part which signifies a whole, namely the resurrection of Christ. He tells us that this is a particular example of a kind of sign, called a *synecdoche*, in which the part can either be read for the whole, or the whole for the part.'[8]

- John Gilchrist says, 'Furthermore we must also note that the figure of speech, as used in Hebrew, always had the same number of days and nights. Moses fasted forty days and forty nights (Exod. 24:18). Jonah was in the [fish] three days and three nights (Jonah 1:17). Job's friends sat with him seven days and seven nights (Job 2:13). We can see that no Jew would have spoken of "seven days and six nights" or "three days and two nights", even if this was the period he was describing. The colloquialism always spoke of an equal number of days and nights and, if a Jew wished to speak of a period of three days which covered only two nights, he would have to speak of three days and three nights. A fine example of this is found in the Book of Esther where the queen said that no one was to eat or drink for three days, night or day (Esth. 4:16) but on the third day, when only two nights had passed, she went into the king's chamber and the fast was ended. So we see quite plainly that "three days and three nights", in Jewish terminology, did not necessarily imply a full period of three actual days and three actual nights but was simply a colloquialism used to cover any part of the first and third days.'[9]

Thus, when Jesus told the Jews He would be three days and three nights in the earth, they took this to mean that the fulfilment of the prophecy could be expected after only two nights. Note that on the day *after* His crucifixion—that is, after only one night (Friday)—they went to Pilate and said, 'Sir, we remember, while He was still alive, how that deceiver said, "After three days I will rise." Therefore command that the tomb be made secure until the third day' (Matt. 27:63–64). The Jewish hierarchy clearly feared that His body might shortly go missing.

Conclusion

The Easter story is the story of God's love for this fallen world, and the resurrection is the triumph of Jesus Christ over 'the last enemy', which is death. Christ has defeated Satan who had the power of death. This power was taken from Satan at the cross (Col. 2:14; Heb. 2:14–15). This is God's solution to death's finality and humiliation for *Homo sapiens*. Because of this, those who repent of their sin and believe in Jesus, trusting in no other Mediator but Jesus Christ alone and no other way to God except by Him, can be confident they will share in the resurrection to come on the Last Day. When the resurrection day arrives, believers will be given a body like the risen Saviour's (John 5:28–29); it will be perfect, fitted for a spiritual existence, and it will have the power of an endless life (1 Cor. 15:50–55). We will share in Christ's victory.

Believing in Jesus justifies sinners: He 'was raised again for our justification' (Rom. 4:25 KJV).[10] There could have been no justification if

Chapter 11

Christ had remained in the tomb. However, the fact that He rose tells us that the work was finished, the price had been paid and God is infinitely satisfied with the sin-atoning work of His Son. This is what the Christian martyrs believed and why they were willing to die. As A. W. Pink put it,

then shall be fulfilled that mystical word, 'I say to you that many will come from east and west, and sit down with Abraham, Isaac, and Jacob in the kingdom of heaven' (Matt. 8:11). As the Lord Jesus declared, 'I lay down My life for the sheep. And other sheep I have which are not of this fold; them also I must bring, and they will hear My voice; and there will be one flock and one shepherd' (John 10:15, 16). Then it shall be that Christ will 'gather *together in one* the children of God who were scattered abroad' (John 11:52)—not only among all nations, but through all dispensations.[11]

The words of Jesus at the tomb of Lazarus challenge us to believe: 'I am the resurrection and the life. He who believes in Me, though he may die, he shall live. And whoever lives and believes in Me shall never die. Do you believe this?' (John 11:25–26).

NOTES

1 Patrick Sookhdeo, *Is the Muslim Isa the Biblical Jesus?* (McLean, VA: Isaac Publishing, 2012), p. 8.

2 *The Gospel of Barnabas*, ed. Aisha Bawany (Karachi: Ashram Publications, 1976), quoted in Peter G. Riddell and Peter Cotterell, *Islam in Conflict: Past, Present and Future* (Leicester: IVP, 2003), pp. 78–79. The Ahmadis teach that Jesus was crucified and was taken down alive and resuscitated in the cold tomb with the help of Nicodemus. He subsequently went East and died and was buried in Kashmir (ibid., pp. 79–80). John Gilchrist concludes, 'No one knows who actually wrote the Gospel of Barnabas but what is known, without a shadow of a doubt, is that whoever it was, it was certainly not the Apostle Barnabas. It was probably a Muslim in Spain who, being the victim of the reconquest of his country, decided to take private revenge by composing a false Gospel under the assumed name of Barnabas.' *Origins and Sources of the Gospel of Barnabas* (Sheffield: Fellowship of Faith for the Muslims, 1992), p. 29.

3 J. C. Ryle, Expository *Thoughts on the Gospel of John*, Vol. 3 (London: James Clarke & Co., 1996). Ryle reckons that there were eleven appearances in total.

4 This was perhaps the risen Christ's fifth appearance (see John 20:19).

5 See ch. 8 in my book *The Real Lord's Prayer* (Leominster: Day One, 2012).

6 H. H. P. Dressler, 'The Sabbath in the Old Testament', in D. Carson (ed.), *From Sabbath to the Lord's Day: A Biblical, Historical and Theological Investigation* (Grand Rapids, MI: Zondervan, 1982), p. 31.

7 Ahmed Deedat, 'What Was the Sign of Jonah?', accessed March 2012, www.islamworld. net/jonah.html. According to Tafsir Ibn Kathir (the most respected Quran commentary among Muslims) on Jonah, Sura Al-Saffat 37:139–143: Muslims 'differed as to how long he spent in the belly of the fish. Some said three days; this was the view of Qatadah. Some said seven days; this was the view of Ja'far As-Sadiq, may Allah be pleased with him. Some said forty days; this was the view of Abu Malik. Mujahid said, narrating from Ash-Sha'bi, "It swallowed him in the morning and cast him forth in the evening." And Allah knows best how long exactly.' Quran Tafsir Ibn Kathir, http://www.qtafsir.com/index.php?option=com_content&task=view&id=1927.

8 Chad Pecknold, 'Reading the Sign of Jonah: A Commentary on Our Biblical Reasoning', *The Journal of Scriptural Reasoning* 3, no. 1 (June 2003), at https://jsr.shanti.virginia.edu/back-issues/vol-3-no-1-extending-the-signs-jonah-in-scriptural-reasoning/reading-the-sign-of-jonah-a-commentary-on-our-biblical-reasoning/.

9 John Gilchrist, 'What Indeed Was the Sign of Jonah?', Answering Islam, accessed March 2012, http://answeringislam.org/Gilchrist/jonah.html.

10 NKJV: 'because of our [need for] justification'.

11 A. W. Pink, *An Exposition of Hebrews* (Grand Rapids, MI: Baker, 1979), p. 891.

The heavenly ministry of Jesus

The LORD said to my Lord,
'Sit at My right hand,
Till I make Your enemies Your footstool.' (Ps. 110:1)

The four Gospels complete the definitive history of the life and work of Jesus Christ while the book of Acts records the history of the New Testament church, beginning with the ascension of the risen Lord Jesus Christ into heaven forty days after His resurrection from the dead:

Now when He had spoken these things, while they watched, He was taken up, and a cloud received Him out of their sight. And while they looked steadfastly toward heaven as He went up, behold, two men stood by them in white apparel, who also said, 'Men of Galilee, why do you stand gazing up into heaven? This same Jesus, who was taken up from you into heaven, will so come in like manner as you saw Him go into heaven.' (Acts 1:9–11)

The ascension of Jesus Christ into heaven

Following the crucifixion and resurrection of Jesus, all that is recorded in the book of Acts and all that the church does for the glory of God is dependent on the doctrine of the ascension of Christ Jesus into heaven to sit at the right hand of the Father (Heb. 1:3). The ascension means that the risen Saviour is now our heavenly Advocate (1 John 2:1). In heaven Jesus Christ continues His High Priestly office praying for the redeemed:

'Christ . . . is also risen, who is even at the right hand of God, who also makes intercession for us' (Rom. 8:34).

The ascension took place ten days before the outpouring of the Holy Spirit at Pentecost. If Jesus had not ascended the 'Helper' (*Paraclete*) would not have come from God. Jesus said that He must go away in order for the Spirit to descend on the church and give gifts to men: 'Nevertheless I tell you the truth. It is to your advantage that I go away; for if I do not go away, the Helper will not come to you; but if I depart, I will send Him to you' (John 16:7). His ascension into heaven thus granted the church its unique authority, equipping it for its ongoing ministry, and guarantees its final victory.

Jesus ascended to the Majesty on high to be crowned with glory and honour (John 17:5) and by doing so He exalted human nature and took it into the realms of glory previously forbidden it. At the resurrection, believers will share in the glory of Christ (but not His essential nature as God). In heaven He is attended by

ten thousand times ten thousand, and thousands of thousands [of the angelic spirits who worship Him], saying with a loud voice,

'Worthy is the Lamb who was slain

To receive power and riches and wisdom,

And strength and honour and glory and blessing!'

And every creature in heaven and on earth, with the twenty-four elders, give honour and worship to God and the Lamb (Rev. 5:11–13).

Thomas Manton said that Christ's exaltation began at His resurrection and received its accomplishment by His sitting at God's right hand, 'being united with his divine person and given immortality, power, knowledge and grace and made free from infirmities'.[1] In heaven, He is seated and reigning over His church: as the Regent King, He says, 'Whatever you ask in My name, that I will do, that the Father may be glorified in the Son. If you ask anything in My name, I will do it' (John 14:13–14).

Islam rejects the idea that prayers can be made to the risen and ascended Jesus Christ in heaven. This flows from the Muslim denial of His Sonship, His resurrection and His ascension into heaven after forty days. After all, for Muslims, Jesus is just a man! We know they reject the truth that 'He alone became the Son of man, in order that we might become through Him sons of God',[2] saying, 'They are deniers of the truth who say, "God is the Christ, the son of Mary"' (Sura 5:72). This denial is constantly made in both the Quran and the Hadith to press home and fix in the conscience that Islam is the truth.

As Jesus Christ has no place in the Muslim idea of God, who, then, do Muslims pray to? Islam insists that prayer is to be made to Allah alone, and it is to be performed as a religious practice five times a day using set (stinted) prayers with the same form of words every time, always in Arabic (see Sura 5:6; 11:114). However, it is not always the case that God alone is the object of Muslims' prayers. Christian missionary midwives who work in Muslim countries are used to hearing pregnant Muslim woman, while in the physical efforts of childbirth, praying for help from Muhammad himself, thus making Muhammad a mediator between God and humanity.[3] This does not square with Islamic literature, which insists that 'Prayer in Islam is a direct link between God and the worshipper. There are no intermediaries between God and the worshipper.'[4] Christians, however, *do* have a loving Mediator, and they benefit because Christ Jesus presents His death to God in continual intercession for His people: 'But you have come to . . . Jesus the Mediator of the new covenant, and to the blood of sprinkling that speaks better things than that of Abel' (Heb. 12:22, 24).

The session of Jesus Christ in heaven

Christians pray to their ascended Saviour who is seated at the right hand of the Majesty on high. This office is given to Jesus Christ alone: 'For there is one God and one Mediator between God and men, the Man Christ Jesus, who gave Himself a ransom for all' (1 Tim. 2:5–6a).

Christians believe that Jesus is seated in heaven keeping His people safe by praying for them as their Shepherd King. Following Jesus' death and resurrection the ascended Saviour is committed to interceding for His sheep as proof of His love. His ascension was the forerunner to His intercession at the right hand of God in heaven: 'Christ . . . is also risen, who is even at the right hand of God, who also makes intercession for us' (Rom. 8:34).

The Old Testament prophesied of Jesus Christ's session in heaven: 'The LORD [Jehovah] said to my Lord [Adoni], "Sit at My right hand, till I make Your enemies Your footstool"' (Ps. 110:1). This doctrine is followed up in the New Testament; in Ephesians 1:20 we read that God raised Jesus 'from the dead and seated Him at His right hand in the heavenly places'. Jesus Christ's ascension took Him 'far above all principality and power and might and dominion, and every name that is named, *not only in this age but also in that which is to come*' (Eph. 1:21, my emphasis). Thus it is written, 'Jesus, the author and finisher of our faith, . . . for the joy that was set before Him endured the cross, despising the shame, *and has sat down at the right hand of the throne of God*' (Heb. 12:2, my emphasis). This means that we are to pray 'in My [Jesus Christ's] name' if our prayers are to be answered. His name is the 'password' necessary for us to get access to heaven. Let us remember that our Saviour said, 'Ask, and it will be given to you' (Luke 11:9). Praying in Jesus' name allows the church to continue Jesus' ministry on earth until He comes a second time (John 14:14). When the church asks in Christ's name (John 14:13–14; 15:16; 16:23–24, 26) it will be blessed, as it:

• Continues His activity;
• Claims His authority;
• Calls for His action.[5]

WHAT DOES JESUS PRAY FOR US?

In heaven Jesus prays to the Father. This heavenly ministry of Christ allows Him to 'save to the uttermost those who come to God through Him' because He appears before God for us (Heb. 7:25). Jesus' words to the Apostle Peter in Luke 22:31–32 make clear His (covenant) commitment to Peter, and, by extension, to all the blood-bought people of God, that He will pray for each one in days of temptation and trouble: 'And the Lord said, "Simon, Simon! Indeed, Satan has asked for you, that he may sift you as wheat. But I have prayed for you, that your faith should not fail; and when you have returned to Me, strengthen your brethren."' The Good Shepherd will care for all His sheep. He will ensure that their faith does not fail and that their service to God will continue through the ups and downs of their pilgrimage and ministry.

The people of God can be assured of help and blessing to come. This is because, as the Apostle John put it, they 'have an Advocate with the Father, Jesus Christ the righteous' (1 John 2:1). For God's people, assurance of protection is grounded in Jesus Christ's dying love, and this is made clear in the Gospels.

PSALM 121

Psalm 121 is an Old Testament picture of the Lord's work during His session. The psalmist says with personal faith, 'My help comes from the LORD, who made heaven and earth' (v. 2). In the psalm we are guaranteed that God will keep His children from slipping or failing. And there is a promise of a Guardian who 'shall neither slumber nor sleep' (v. 4), that is, One who is personally involved in their life and work and is committed to the security of all His people, even the most obscure among them. He brings hope with great and precious promises that His sheep will be sheltered from every evil power because their Guardian shields them from harm. Day and night protection is poetically described in the words 'The sun shall not strike you by day, nor the moon by night' (v. 6); this is welcome and necessary protection in a world that is fallen and hostile. It is, of course, fundamentally speaking of protection and freedom from all forms of spiritual harm. There is the guarantee of deliverance 'from all evil' (v. 7). His trusting sheep can know that their Messiah is working 'all things together for good to those who love God, to those who are the called according to His purpose' (Rom. 8:28).

Thus we see that Psalm 121 is a prophetic word about Jesus Christ's heavenly session. Here is a guarantee of our Saviour's personal and deep interest in the saints individually. He 'shall preserve your soul' and 'your going out and your coming in from this time forth and even forevermore' (vv. 7–8). From this precious psalm we learn that the Saviour's beloved people are constantly

- Upon His *mind*: He is always thinking of their good (Ps. 119:68);
- In His *heart*: even as Israel's high priest bore the names of the twelve tribes upon his breastplate, so Christ Jesus has all His sheep close to His heart;
- Before His *eyes*: the eyes of the Lord never sleep but are perpetually watching over their welfare.

'Behold, He who keeps Israel shall neither slumber nor sleep' (v. 4).

Conclusion

Jesus Christ's session is good news for sinners and saints alike. Because He lives for ever, 'He is also able to save to the uttermost those who come to God through Him, since He always lives to make intercession for them' (Heb. 7:25). Prayer is an act of faith whereby the soul calls out to the Son of God who has ascended and is seated on high at God's right hand. 'Seeing then that we have a great High Priest who has passed through the heavens, Jesus the Son of God, let us hold fast our confession . . . Let us therefore come boldly to the throne of grace, that we may obtain mercy and find grace to help in time of need' (4:14, 16). This means that God's people are to live their lives 'looking unto Jesus, the author and finisher of our faith, who for the joy that was set before Him endured the cross, despising the shame, and has sat down at the right hand of the throne of God' (12:2).

If Christ Jesus had not ascended and begun His session, the words he spoke to Peter, 'I have prayed for you', could not be applied to all God's adopted children. He sits at the right hand of the Father, interceding to secure for us salvation's full and final adoption (Rom. 8:23). Christ our Saviour, having died for us, sprinkles us with His precious blood to cleanse us. The application of the blood to believers' hearts is by the Spirit, sent forth from the Father and the Son at Christ's request (Heb. 9:14).

The ascension not only took Jesus to heaven but it also secured our eternal place in heaven with Him. When He left this world, Jesus did not forget the sheep for whom He had died. The reigning, loving Christ Jesus is preparing (i.e. securing) a place ('mansions') for all the people of God so they can be with him for ever (John 14). In heavenly session our coming King fulfils the sweet promise that He will never leave us nor forsake us (Matt. 28:20b).

The moment His people breathe their last and leave the world, He will bring them to 'Paradise'. Thus there will be room for *all* those who, by faith in the gospel, have prepared themselves to be with Him. The separation of soul and body (death) is the signal to our ascended Saviour to send heavenly angels to bring the redeemed to His side so that they are with Him in the intermediate state (Luke 16:22; 2 Cor. 5:1–8). At the resurrection of the just on the Last Day the dead in Christ will be raised and will be for ever with the Lord (1 Thes. 4:16–18). The risen and ascended Jesus Christ is the 'forerunner' who brings hope and eternal redemption 'for us' (Heb. 6:20; 9:12). This was the 'joy set before Him' (Heb. 12:2). This was the plan which was prepared in eternity, 'before the foundation of the world' (Matt. 25:34; 1 Peter 1:20). In the light of this, God's people can sing with new understanding the chorus,

Chapter 12

Because He lives, I can face tomorrow;
Because He lives, all fear is gone;
Because I know He holds the future,
And life is worth the living
Just because He lives!
(W. J. Gaither)

NOTES

1 Thomas Manton, *An Exposition of John 17* (Wilmington, DE: Sovereign Grace, 1972), p. 91.
2 Augustine of Hippo, *A Treatise against Two Letters of the Pelagians*, 4.6.
3 This is not official Islam; however, it demonstrates the human awareness of and need for a mediator with God.
4 I. A. Ibrahim, *A Brief Illustrated Guide to Understanding Islam* (Houston: Darussalam, 1996), p. 66.
5 See chs. 2 and 3 in my book *Getting to Grips with Prayer* (Leominster: Day One, 2017).

The Second Coming

Beloved, do not believe every spirit, but test the spirits, whether they are of God; because many false prophets have gone out into the world. (1 John 4:1)

The Muslim view

The Day of Judgement is referred to in the Quran—Suras 7:187; 18:98–99; 34:33–34, 63; 77:11; 99:1–5—though the majority of details are in the Hadith and Sunna. Muslims believe that at the end of the world there will be a 'Day of Resurrection' and after that 'the Day of Judgement' when the annihilation of all life will be followed by its resurrection and judgement by Allah. The Hadith speaks of a Great Tribulation. 'The Day of Judgment is also known as the Day of Reckoning, the Last Day and the Hour.'[1] At the time of judgement, chaos will reign. Jesus and the Mahdi[2] are central characters in the events that will take place at that time. The Mahdi will have established a seven-year rule in Medina, at which time Jesus will descend from heaven and battle against the Islamic Antichrist (see below).

Hadith reference the Mahdi and [Jesus] simultaneously and the return of the Mahdi will coincide with the return of [Jesus], who will descend from the heavens . . . The two will meet, and the Mahdi will lead the people in . . . prayer. After the prayer, they will open a gate to the west and encounter [the Islamic Antichrist]. [The Mahdi and Jesus will triumph and liberate Islam from cruelty.] After the defeat of [the Islamic Antichrist], [Jesus] will lead a peaceful forty-year reign until his death. He will be buried in a tomb beside Muhammad in Medina.

These events will be followed by a time of serenity when people will live according to religious values.

Chapter 13

The believers, the Jews or Christians and the Sabeans—all those who believed in God and the Last Day and do good deeds—will be rewarded by their Lord; they shall have no fear, nor shall they grieve. (Sura 2:62)

Similar to other Abrahamic religions, Islam teaches that there will be a resurrection of the dead that will be followed by a final tribulation and eternal division of the righteous and wicked. Islamic apocalyptic literature describing Armageddon is often known as . . . the Great Massacre . . . The righteous are rewarded with the pleasures of . . . Paradise, while the unrighteous are punished in . . . Hell.

On the Day of Judgement,

the dead will stand in a grand assembly, awaiting a scroll detailing their righteous deeds, sinful acts, and ultimate judgment. Muhammad will be the first to be resurrected . . . Punishments will include . . . severe pain and . . . shame. There will also be a punishment of the grave (for those who disbelieved).

The Christian view

Teaching on the Second Coming of Jesus Christ finds expression throughout the New Testament. If one reads it from cover to cover it will be seen that the New Testament writers believed in this future event. In the book of Revelation we have this prediction: 'Behold, He is coming with clouds, and every eye will see Him, even they who pierced Him. And all the tribes of the earth will mourn because of Him. Even so, Amen' (Rev. 1:7). This is rooted in the prophecies of the Old Testament which point to the Day of the Lord's coming. The church has always loved this teaching because it brings encouragement, hope and comfort (1 Thes. 4:18). The Bible says that at the revealing of the Lord Jesus Christ, He will return with his angels (Matt. 13:30, 41; 24:31), the world will be burned up and the wicked will be judged (see 2 Peter 3:10–13). Those who will be judged are described as 'those who do not know God' (2 Thes. 1:8), because they have remained unrepentant all their lives; yet the Bible makes it clear that Jesus Christ came to introduce us to the Father so we will gain eternal life (John 17:3). The Greek word which is translated 'coming' in 2 Thessalonians 2:1, 8 is also happily translated 'presence'. When Christ Himself comes He will be present with us.

Paul's epistle 1 Thessalonians gives details of the events that will precede the Parousia (the Second Coming) which are not easy to understand. Christians are divided as to the interpretation and unbelievers are perplexed by the language used. Evangelical believers, however, all agree that Jesus Christ is coming back *personally* and this is the essential issue when it comes to the Second Coming of the Saviour: 'the Lord *Himself* will descend with a shout' (1 Thes. 4:16, my emphasis). Christians expect a personal, visible return of the Lord Jesus Christ.

At the most simple level there are three main views of the end times held by evangelicals, with a fourth variant based on the third view:

- *Amillennialism:* this view holds that the millennium of Revelation 20 is not to be understood literally and that the thousand years are symbolic of the time from the cross of Christ to the Second Coming. During this time Christ reigns from heaven, the gospel is preached to all the nations, the church is in the midst of tribulation and Israel will be converted before the Second Coming. At the Second Coming, there will be the 'rapture' of the saints, the general resurrection and the final judgement. Then the new heavens and earth will be ushered in.
- *Postmillennialism:* in this view the millennium is a period of earthly blessedness that precedes the Second Coming of Christ. The millennial period, however, may or may not last a literal thousand years. Before Christ comes the gospel will be more effective, with the conversion of the nations and the Jews, and a long period of righteousness and peace will ensue. After this, Satan will be

loosed, bringing great tribulation and apostasy, and the Antichrist will appear. At the end of the millennium there will be the general resurrection and final judgement. Then the new heavens and earth will be ushered in.

- *Historic premillennialism:* this view believes that there will be a literal thousand-year reign of Christ on earth before the final judgement. At the Second Coming believers will be raised from the dead (the first resurrection), living saints will be 'raptured', the righteous judged, the Antichrist slain and the Jews converted. During the Millennial Kingdom, Jesus will reign with the saints at Jerusalem, while unbelieving nations will be kept in check. This will be a time of social justice and peace, and Satan will be bound for a thousand years. At the last judgement unbelievers will be raised from the dead (the second resurrection) and judged. Then the new heavens and earth will be ushered in.

- *Dispensational premillennialism:* an extension of historic premillennialism, this view takes a strong literalist view of Old Testament prophecy. A dispensation is 'a period of time during which man is tested in respect to his obedience to some specific revelation of the will of God' (New Scofield Bible). This view holds to a fundamental and abiding distinction between Israel and the church and divides time into seven periods beginning at creation and ending at the millennium. It believes that after the great tribulation (which will last three and a half years), the second stage of the coming of Christ will introduce the millennium. This is believed to be the fulfilment of Daniel's seventieth week ending the great tribulation, with the destruction of Antichrist, the binding of Satan for a thousand years and the restoration of Israel. At the last judgement the unsaved of all ages will be raised from the dead, after which the heavenly New Jerusalem will descend to earth.

In spite of their differences the three views at their most *basic* are very similar. The diagram shows this.

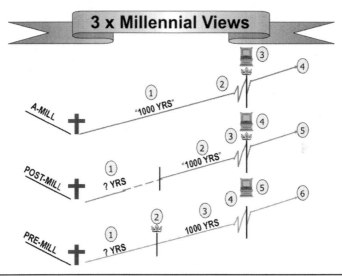

KEY TO CHART			
	Amillennial	**Postmillennial**	**Premillennial**
1.	Non-literal unknown time scale	Unknown time scale	Unknown time scale
2.	Second Coming of Jesus	'1,000'-year reign (not necessarily literal)	Second Coming of Jesus with the 'rapture'—part 1
3.	The great white throne: Judgement Day	Second Coming of Jesus	1,000-year reign: the millennium
4.	The new heavens and earth	The great white throne: Judgement Day	Second Coming of Jesus —part 2
5.	–	The new heavens and earth	The great white throne: Judgement Day
6.	–	–	The new heavens and earth

Chapter 13

The Antichrist

AN ISLAMIC VIEW

The Islamic Antichrist (*ad-Dajjal*) does not appear in the Quran but is a prominent figure in Hadith and Islamic eschatology as a whole. He appears gruesome and is blind in his right eye. He will gain followers through his miracle-working and apparent wealth and generosity. It is believed that he will appear prior to the Day of Judgement, when he will engage in an epic battle with, and be killed by, Jesus.[3]

NEW TESTAMENT VIEW

The Antichrist is described in 2 Thessalonians 2 as 'the man of sin' and 'the son of perdition':

Let no one deceive you by any means; for that Day will not come unless the falling away comes first, and the man of sin is revealed, the son of perdition, who opposes and exalts himself above all that is called God or that is worshiped, so that he sits as God in the temple of God, showing himself that he is God. (vv. 3–4)

In the events prior to the Saviour's coming the Antichrist will play a prominent part. Paul had told the Thessalonian believers about the rise of the Antichrist when he was with them at Thessalonica, but he also wrote it down for them, encouraging them to remember that believers will be safely gathered together to Christ out of harm's way (2 Thes. 2:5).

IDENTITY OF THE ANTICHRIST[4]

In Christianity's early days the Antichrist was identified variously as the spirit of heresy (by Polycarp), the Roman Empire (by Irenaeus) or the resurrected Nero (by John Chrysostom).[5] Some in the Roman Catholic Church considered the Antichrist to be the Holy Roman Emperor Frederick II (1194–1250). In more recent times, the German warmonger

Adolf Hitler and the Egyptian Anwar Sadat have been nominated. Today the idea that the Antichrist may be the Secretary-General of the United Nations is mooted, while some think that the coming Antichrist will probably be Jewish, and that he will be from the tribe of Dan. These latter ideas come from those who hold a futurist interpretation of Bible prophecy.[6]

Historically, the Antichrist has been considered an apostate priest or Christian secular ruler, perhaps a pope or other high leader of the Christian church. Many amillennial scholars hold to the idea that the Roman Papacy fulfils this prophecy and that the succession of popes who rose to power in Rome following the fall of the Roman Empire in AD 410 meets the profile of the power that is 'restraining' (2 Thes. 2:6). This view was shared by John Wycliffe, Jan Hus, Martin Luther, John Calvin, John Knox, Zwingli, G. Fox, B. W. Newton and John Wesley, and is contained in the Westminster Confession of Faith, the Savoy Declaration and the Baptist Confession of Faith of 1689.

Another view concerning the Antichrist

finds its understanding based in its overall view of the Book of Revelation. Those who ascribe to this theory believe that the Book of Revelation is not simply predicting what will happen at the end of time, but is also describing what is always happening upon the earth. In this view, each generation has an Antichrist that the faithful will identify and defeat through exposing his evil.[7]

All this shows how difficult it is to clearly define the identity of the Antichrist. Christians need to watch and wait patiently for Christ's Second Coming (Matt. 24:42–44). Perhaps we should accept that God has kept some things unclear. What is clear, however, is the statement of the Apostle John in the first century AD: 'Who is a liar but he who denies that Jesus is the Christ? He is antichrist who denies the Father and the

Son. Whoever denies the Son does not have the Father either; he who acknowledges the Son has the Father also' (1 John 2:22–23).

Conclusion

There are many similarities between the Islamic tradition concerning the Day of Judgement and the New Testament text. It would not be out of the way to think that Islam's teaching mimics that of the New Testament. In the Christian Scriptures, the Second Coming of Jesus is the continuation of God's plan of redemption. Jesus' incarnation, resurrection and ascension are the harbingers of the Parousia to come:

if we believe that Jesus died and rose again, even so God will bring with Him those who sleep in Jesus. For this we say to you by the word of the Lord, that we who are alive and remain until the coming of the Lord will by no means precede those who are asleep. For the Lord Himself will descend from heaven with a shout, with the voice of an archangel, and with the trumpet of God. And the dead in Christ will rise first. Then we who are alive and remain shall be caught up together with them in the clouds to meet the Lord in the air. And thus we shall always be with the Lord. Therefore comfort one another with these words. (1 Thes. 4:14–18)

The Second Coming of Christ, described as 'the day of the Lord' (1 Thes. 5:2), is the moment in history when God shall vindicate His Son and all the redeemed who have believed unto eternal life. Paul makes this point: '. . . when He comes, in that Day, to be glorified in His saints and to be admired among all those who believe' (2 Thes. 1:10). At the Last Day God will reveal His people to the universe as His children (Rom. 8:18–23; Phil. 2:9–11) and Christ will share His glory with them. They will be for ever with the Lord when 'that Day' comes.

Saviour, hasten Thine appearing!
Bring, O bring the glorious day,

When, the awful summons hearing,
Heaven and earth shall pass away!
Then with golden harps we'll sing,
'Gory, glory to our King!'
(Thomas Kelly, 'Hark! Ten Thousand Harps and Voices', 1806)

NOTES

1 'Islamic Eschatology', Wikipedia, https://en.wikipedia.org/wiki/Islamic_eschatology. Other quotations are from this source.

2 Mahdi: the 'rightly guided one', whose return is awaited by Shia Muslims. See Patrick Sookhdeo, *A Pocket Guide to Islam* (Fern, Ross-shire: Christian Focus / Isaac Publishing, 2010), p. 118. The existence of the Mahdi is not an established doctrine of Islam but many Sunni do expect him; for Shia Muslims he is a reappearance of their twelfth Imam.

3 'Islamic Eschatology'.

4 See my book *Opening Up 2 Thessalonians* (Leominster: Day One, 2008).

5 'Antichrist', Wikipedia, https://en.wikipedia.org/wiki/Antichrist.

6 Futurists hold to a literal view of prophecy.

7 Source unknown.

Cults and new religions

Then if anyone says to you, 'Look, here is the Christ!' or 'There!' do not believe it. For false christs and false prophets will rise and show great signs and wonders to deceive, if possible, even the elect. See, I have told you beforehand. Therefore if they say to you, 'Look, He is in the desert!' do not go out; or 'Look, He is in the inner rooms!' do not believe it. (Matt. 24:23–26)

All cults, whether within the broad scope of Christianity or otherwise, add a source of authority which in their belief system replaces and reinterprets Holy Scripture and supersedes both its authority and sufficiency. A cult is defined as 'a system of religious belief; a sect; an unorthodox or false religion; a great, often excessive, admiration for a person or idea; the person or idea giving rise to such admiration'.[1] The Christian Scriptures tell us that many will try to imitate and supersede Jesus Christ as God's Apostle and Saviour of humankind. This will be attempted by false prophets. Some false prophets last but for a moment while others last for an age. Some are self-appointed while others have trusting followers. Some are local while others are regional, national or universal. Some are new while others are ancient. However they present themselves, we are to watch out for them and reject them and their teachings as false (i.e. counterfeit imitations of the real and true Word of God) if the faith of the church is rejected. Our Lord Himself warned about false prophets (Matt. 24:23–26).

What are the marks of a cult?
Firstly, cults place their ultimate authority not in the Bible alone but in some non-scriptural source. So they have mixed feelings about the Bible, on the one hand wanting to appear as a valid godly religion but, on the other hand, wanting to alter the plain meaning of the text of Scripture. A

cult always puts the teaching of its founder before the teachings of Jesus and Christ's inspired apostles and the forty or so biblical writers. Thus their teachings do not come from the Bible alone but represent a mixture of biblical and non-biblical sources: light and darkness to produce a dark shade of grey. However, the Bible itself says that no new teaching is required as it is through the voice and teachings (doctrines) of Jesus Christ that God has spoken (Matt. 5:17–18; John 10:35; 2 Tim. 3:15–16; Heb. 1:1–2; 1 Peter 1:25; 2 Peter 1:19–21; 3:2, 16).

Secondly, the way of salvation taught within a cult sets aside the doctrine of justification by grace alone through faith alone as found in the Scriptures of the Old and New Testaments, replacing it with rules and regulations which are said to gain merit with God. Such teaching believes that salvation is the reward for keeping the commandments of God as defined by the cult. The doctrine of justification by faith alone, however, was central to the gospel which the apostles preached. In the Epistle to the Romans Paul expounds the way of salvation, stating that it does not depend on human acts of obedience to God's laws or kindness and charity to others, but is the free gift of God's grace given to all who believe in God's Redeemer Jesus Christ: 'For what does the Scripture say? "Abraham believed God, and it was accounted to him for righteousness." Now to him who works, the wages are not counted as grace but as debt. But to him who does not work but believes on Him who justifies the ungodly, his faith is accounted for righteousness' (Rom. 4:3–5).

Thirdly, all cults share in a devaluation of the Person of Christ Jesus and depreciation of His Work of atonement. They like to shift the emphasis which the Bible puts on His Person and His Work, by rejecting His divine Sonship and equality with God the Father. Most say that Christ was created by God, and may have been an angel endowed with immortality. One teaches that He was only different from us in degree and not kind, saying that He along with Adam and Joseph Smith created the earth. Another believes that the Son 'existed potentially in the divine will'. The Bible, however, shows that Christ was God and man in one person with two natures (John 17:5; Phil. 2:6–8; 1 Tim. 3:16; Heb. 1:6–8; 1 Peter 1:2; 1 John 1:3).

Fourthly, each cult regards itself as the people of God on earth. It is convinced that it is the only true and faithful community of God's people. Church history is easy for the cults as they claim that nothing of real significance happened to the church between the time of the apostles and the founding of their cult. They alone are God's true people; all others without exception are followers of the devil. The cults, however, have no appreciation of the biblical doctrine of 'one holy catholic church' (i.e. the universal church) composed of Christ's true people of all ages and all nations, irrespective of colour or people group (John 17:20–21; 1 Cor. 12; Eph. 4:3–7; 5:25–27; 1 John 2:1–2; Rev. 7:9).

Fifthly, some cults do not believe in the Second Coming of Christ at all. But all of them place themselves at the very centre of things at the world's end. They are convinced God has called their group into existence and that its birth marks the climax of history. Common to all cults is their belief that at the apocalyptic end of the world *they* will finally triumph in the sight of the entire universe and be vindicated at the end.

Islam today

What has this to tell us about Islam as seen today? The *shahadah* (the Islamic creed) states, 'No Deity but Allah and Muhammad is the messenger of Allah'. Quranic teaching represents a mixture of Old and New Testament content and some non-biblical sources from Zoroastrianism (Iranian) producing a new and different worldview from the Judaeo-Christian ethos. Islam claims it holds to the monotheism that originally came down from the Old Testament prophets and messengers. It also asserts that all references to Muhammad were removed by Jews and Christians changing the Bible text. Thus, 'based on these claims, the Quran proceeds to reconstruct the lives and messages of the Biblical characters to develop key Islamic doctrines, while opposing the original

Biblical ones'.[2] It has built new narratives about Abraham, Isaac and Jacob, saying that they were all Muslims (Suras 3:68, 84). The claim that Jews and Christians have changed their Scriptures is so ingrained in the Muslim psyche that when it comes to the gospel they reject it out of hand.

ISLAM'S ULTIMATE AUTHORITY IS NOT THE SCRIPTURES

Islam's ultimate authority is not the Scriptures of the people of the Book but the Quran, the Hadith and consensus. The Quran is regarded as God's (Allah's) final message to the world given to Muhammad when he was visited by a heavenly messenger during the last twenty-three years of his life. As we saw earlier, it was written down from memory by Muhammad's followers on hearing it, 'on various things such as leather, camel bone, stone, leaves, wood or even tree bark'.[3] These fragments were collected between AD 650 and 656 by the caliph Uthman and bound into a book in the Arabic language.[4] This being complete, all the fragments were destroyed.[5] It is made up of 114 chapters called suras arranged in order of length, from the shortest to the longest (except for Sura 1). The Quran is treated with the utmost respect and cannot be written on or put on the ground. Islam teaches its followers that the Quran is an exact copy, word for word, of a Quran which has existed for ever in heaven.[6] It is their holy book. Islam is quick to claim as its own the Bible's great prophets—Noah (Nooh), Abraham (Ibrahim), Moses (Moosa) and even Jesus (Isa)—but it gives them a new history and destiny. This cannot be accepted by Christians: it holds no reality and has no biblical warrant.

ISLAM'S WAY OF SALVATION IS DIFFERENT

The way of salvation through the merits of Jesus Christ taught in the Bible is replaced with Islamic rules which gain merit with God. These are the obligatory duties called the 'Five Pillars of Islam':

1. *Confessing the faith* (*shahadah*), that is, 'I testify that there is no god but Allah and that Muhammad is the Apostle of Allah',

asserting Allah as the one deity and Muhammad as the final prophet of Allah;

2. *Prayer* five times a day facing towards Mecca and at midday Friday in the mosque;

3. *Fasting* during the daylight hours in the twenty-eight days of the month of Ramadan, the ninth month in the Islamic calendar;

4. *Almsgiving* to the poor of Islam—*at least* 2.5 per cent of one's wealth;

5. *Pilgrimage* to Mecca: the Muslim must undertake the *hajj* at least once in their lifetime.

A significant minority propose that a sixth pillar, namely Jihad, be added. The term literally means 'striving' but it 'has a variety of interpretations including (i) spiritual struggle for moral purity, (ii) trying to correct wrong and support right by words and actions, [and] (iii) military war in the name of Allah, against non-Muslims with the aim of spreading Islam, against apostates from Islam, or against Muslims with unorthodox theology'.[7]

To become a Muslim one has to repeat the *shahadah* (Islamic creed) three times in front of two witnesses. Christians ask, Is this good enough for God? How can a sinner be accepted by the holy and eternal God and become right with God? Islam, like all cults, rejects the concept of God's free grace and the power of the new birth to change lives and hearts, substituting these with good works and human merit. Obedience to the Quran's teachings and the way of life that Islam's 'Five Pillars' dictate gains favour. The very meaning of the word 'Muslim' is one who submits himself in unquestioning obedience to Allah's will. 'When someone converts to Islam, God forgives all of his previous sins and evil deeds. The Prophet said: didn't you know that converting to Islam erases all previous sins?'[8] However, the gospel is clear:

When I see the blood, I will pass over you. (Exod. 12:13)

... redeemed ... with the precious blood of Christ, as of a lamb without blemish and without spot. (1 Peter 1:19)

For by grace you have been saved through faith, and that not of yourselves; it is the gift of God, not of works, lest anyone should boast. (Eph. 2:8–9; see also Gal. 1:8)

If we confess our sins, He is faithful and just to forgive us our sins and to cleanse us from all unrighteousness. (1 John 1:9)

ISLAM DEVALUES THE PERSON OF CHRIST AND HIS WORK

Muslims like to shift the emphasis which the Bible puts on Jesus Christ's Person and Work, by rejecting His divine Sonship and equality with God the Father. Islam vehemently rejects the Bible's clear claim that Jesus Christ is the Second Person of the Holy Trinity. What do the Scriptures say?

The Second Epistle of the Apostle John is written to 'the elect lady and her children'. Here John elaborates on his statement regarding Jesus' union with the Father: 'Grace, mercy, and peace will be with you from God the Father and from the Lord Jesus Christ, the Son of the Father, in truth and love' (2 John 3). The extra phrase 'the Son of the Father' is carefully inserted as John is keen to back up his teaching on the deity of the incarnate Redeemer Jesus Christ, lest there be any doubt in the elect lady's mind, or indeed in her children's minds, that Christ is God the Son incarnate in the flesh. This doctrine is also clear from our Lord's own words in his High Priestly prayer recorded in John 17:4–5: 'I have glorified You on the earth. I have finished the work which You have given Me to do. And now, O Father, glorify Me together with Yourself, with the glory which I had with You before the world was.' Christians believe that God's Son, the Second Person of the Trinity, is the Saviour of the world, and since His resurrection and ascension into heaven He rules His church by the Holy Spirit and by the 'external Word' the Bible (as Martin Luther would have it).[9] While on earth, Jesus Christ warned His followers that after His death and resurrection there would be those who would challenge and oppose His gospel, claiming messianic and prophetic authority for themselves. History has shown this to be true.

ISLAM REGARDS ITSELF AS THE PEOPLE OF GOD ON EARTH

Islam is convinced that it is the only true and faithful community of God's people. The *Ummah* (the community of Islam) sees itself as the special people of God. Muhammad's example is to be followed because he is said to have been directed by Allah. In spite of the fact that Islam is around 700 years younger than Christianity, it replaces Jesus Christ with Muhammad as God's chief apostle. Its teachings powerfully bind the conscience into believing that those who confess Muhammad to be 'the Apostle of God' are Allah's chosen people. One of the consequences of this attitude is the desire to impose sharia law on all nations.[10] This is a legal, political and religious system developed from the Quran and the Hadith. This can be accomplished using violence and war (Islamic history is evidence of this policy). The teaching of Jihad instructs Muslims to kill non-Muslims to achieve domination and gain eternal divine reward without offending Allah. In Islamic countries, or those with a majority of Muslims, sharia is imposed with the effect that Christians and Jews are treated as second-class citizens. Converts to Christianity are often discriminated against and persecuted.[11] This intolerance flows from the attitude that the *Ummah* must bring all peoples and nations to submission to the will of Allah whatever the cost.

THE ISLAMIC VIEW OF THE DAY OF JUDGEMENT IS DIFFERENT

As we saw in the last chapter, the Islamic view of the Day of Judgement is found mainly in the Hadith and involves Jesus returning to earth as a Muslim! The Islamic Antichrist (*ad-Dajjal*) will appear and be helped by the Jews. He will deceive many by miracles and false doctrines. However, Jesus Christ is not the Saviour but another, called the Mahdi, will lead the battle and fight Gog and Magog (Sura 21:95–96), eventually restoring Islam to its original glory with Jesus' help. When Jesus returns to earth as a Muslim, he will break the cross, kill all pigs, convert all Christians to Islam and all the Jews will be killed. The returned Jesus will reign with the Mahdi for forty years, marry, have children, then die and be buried next to Muhammad.[12]

When the Day of Judgement comes, all non-Muslims will go to hell; some Muslims will spend time in hell before going to Paradise. Hell is torment, while Paradise is full of wonderful things and 'much sexual activity'.[13] The Mahdi is not Muhammad, nor is he mentioned in the Quran; he is an eschatological figure of Islamic tradition (Hadith) who is predicted to rule the world with Jesus' help at His Second Coming. The Mahdi is Islam's eschatological redeemer who will create a just social order based on Islamic ideas and be the Caliph and Imam of the Muslim world. This new world order will be established in Islam's usual way by military action against all those who oppose it. The Mahdi will conquer Israel and lead the 'faithful Muslims' in a final slaughter and battle against Jews. Islam will be the only religion practised on the earth.[14] 'The believers, the Jews, Christians and the Sabeans—all those who believe in God and the Last Day and do good deeds—will be rewarded by their Lord; they shall have no fear, nor shall they grieve' (Sura 2:62).

Conclusion

For Christians, Islam is not the true religion of God. Christian believers are assured by God the Spirit that Jesus who came into the world taking the form of a man was also God, and that the Scriptures of the Old and New Testaments are the Word of God to the world offering forgiveness, cleansing and adoption in the name of Jesus Christ alone to all who believe. This is what the Epistle of Paul to the Philippians makes clear:

[Christ Jesus,] being in the form of God, did not consider it robbery to be equal with God, but made Himself of no reputation, taking the form of a bondservant, and coming in the likeness of men. And being found in appearance as a man, He humbled Himself and became obedient to the point of death, even the death of the cross. Therefore God also has highly exalted Him and given Him the name which is above every name, that at the name of Jesus every knee should bow, of those in heaven, and of those on earth, and of those under the earth, and that every tongue should confess that Jesus Christ is Lord, to the glory of God the Father. (Phil. 2:6–11)

NOTES

1 *The Chambers Thesaurus*, 2004, © Chambers Harrap Publishers Ltd.

2 Sam Solomon, *Not the Same God* (London: Wilberforce Publications, 2016), p. 89.

3 Barnabas Fund, *Unveiled: A Christian Study Guide to Islam* (McLean, VA: Isaac Publishing, 2011), p. 44.

4 Ibid., p. 45. The Arabic Kufic script had no vowels and no punctuation. Muhammad died in AD 632.

5 Ibid.

6 Ibid. The Quran is only the Book of God in Arabic. All translations are interpretations.

7 Patrick Sookhdeo, *A Pocket Guide to Islam* (Fern, Ross-shire: Christian Focus / Isaac Publishing, 2010), p. 117.

8 Ibrahim, *A Brief Illustrated Guide to Understanding Islam* (Houston: Darussalam, 1996), p. 44.

9 'The saving, sanctifying, illuminating Spirit of God, he [Luther] says, comes to us through this "external Word" [the Bible].' John Piper, *The Legacy of Sovereign Joy* (Leicester: IVP, 2000), p. 78.

10 The two main divisions within Islam are Sunni and Shia. Almost 90 per cent are Sunni. They believe that sharia—Islamic law—can never be changed.

11 See 'Dawa through Jihad and Violence', chs. 9 and 10 in Patrick Sookhdeo, *Dawa: The Islamic Strategy for Reshaping the Modern World* (McLean, VA: Isaac Publishing, 2014).

12 Barnabas Fund, *Unveiled*, p. 52.

13 Ibid., p. 52.

14 'The Mahdi: Islam's Awaited Messiah', Answering Islam, http://www.answering-islam.org/Authors/JR/Future/ch04_the_mahdi.htm.

The challenge of Islam

Many false prophets will rise up and deceive many. (Matt. 24:11)

I
n both the Old and New Testaments the Bible speaks about false
prophets. Deceptive visions which present false prophecies and
delusions are condemned:

Your prophets have seen for you
False and deceptive visions. (Lam. 2:14)

The prophets prophesy lies in My name. I have not sent them, commanded them, nor
spoken to them; they prophesy to you a false vision, divination, a worthless thing, and
the deceit of their heart. Therefore thus says the LORD concerning the prophets who
prophesy in My name, whom I did not send . . . 'By sword and famine those prophets
shall be consumed!' (Jer. 14:14–15)

Beloved, do not believe every spirit, but test the spirits, whether they are of God;
because many false prophets have gone out into the world. (1 John 4:1)

Christians are to test the spirits to see whether they are of God
because of the false prophets in every age and nation. This testing is to
be done on the foundation of the doctrines of the Bible and a biblical
worldview (1 John 2:26). The Holy Scriptures are the touchstone of
true religion. In 1 John 2:22 we note that the Apostle John's passion and
goal is to lift Jesus high and to let the world know about His Work and
the glory of His Person, as well as making sure the church is clear about
Christ's equality with the Father.

Honour the Son

The church must be clear about the answer to the question: who was Jesus Christ? Some views of Jesus place Him among the great religious teachers of this world. There can be no doubt that He has influenced billions, changed the course of history and moulded the character of nations like the UK and USA and continents like Europe. But does that view do Him justice? C. S. Lewis presented three choices in answer to this question: either Jesus was mad, bad or God. Others have expressed it thus: Jesus Christ was either a lunatic, a liar or the Lord.

So who was Jesus? Not an angel, not a great Jewish teacher, not a hoaxer, not a mistake of history, but rather the Second Person of the Trinity incarnate, the promised Messiah. He changes minds and hearts for His kingdom is within those who believe on Him (Matt. 3:2; 5:3; 6:10, 33; 7:21; 13:44; Luke 17:21).[1] The Gospels show that Jesus accepted worship, forgave sins and spoke of His eternal Sonship.

Jesus was true God from 'the beginning' (John 1:1–33). The New Testament teaches that there was not a time when Christ did not exist. Paul expressed his wonder at this by saying,

> And without controversy great is the mystery of godliness:
> God was manifested in the flesh,
> Justified in the Spirit,
> Seen by angels,
> Preached among the Gentiles,
> Believed on in the world,
> Received up in glory. (1 Tim. 3:16)

The glory and equality of Jesus was pre-creation and pre-incarnation glory. It was before the world was. Thus the Bible teaches the 'Trinitarian Son'. Christians therefore contend that Jesus Christ is to be accepted as the eternal Son of God because this is taught in the Scriptures. The Gospel of John is key: 'all should honor the Son just as they honor the Father. He who does not honor the Son does not honor the Father who sent Him' (John 5:23). Paul points this reality out in his First Epistle to the Corinthians: 'for us there is one God, the Father, of whom are all things, and we for Him; and one Lord Jesus Christ, through whom are all things, and through whom we live' (1 Cor. 8:6).

Antichrist

The Bible calls Islam's denial and rejection of Jesus as the Son of God 'antichrist': 'Who is a liar but he who denies that Jesus is the Christ? He is antichrist who denies the Father and the Son' (1 John 2:22). Some of the ideas mooted in Islam come from sources before Muhammad. Gnostic writings and philosophical works of men opposed to the basic tenets of the whole Bible (Old and New Testaments alike) must have been influential in Muhammad's thinking. Islam did not simply arise out of nowhere; there was a context to its origins, partly led by Muhammad's rejection of paganism and polytheism and his belief in monotheism. As Tom Holland says, 'To understand the origins of Islam, and why it evolved the way that it did we must look far beyond the age of Ibn Hisham (Mohammed). We must explore the empires and religions of late antiquity.' 'The soil out of which Islam sprung was one full of a prodigious number of gods.'[2] Islam's purpose was to preach monotheism and at the same time to invent *another* way of salvation which is *not* another (see Gal. 1).

Islam maintains, on the strength of the Quran, that the Bible does not contain the actual words of Jesus, but rather words of others about him (Sura 2:75, 78–79). It claims, on the other hand, that the Quran is a miraculous document having no errors or changes since its origin. However, 'Muslims cannot offer any convincing historical evidence . . . they cannot explain who changed the New Testament. Or when, or where.'[3] The New Testament relies on some 5,686 Greek manuscript copies in existence today together with ancient Syriac, Latin and Coptic versions, as well as other versions of the New Testament; also there are Patristic quotations from the New Testament to ascertain its original content. Bruce Metzger notes, 'The textual critic of the New Testament is embarrassed by the wealth of his material.'[4] Muslim authors fail to give the Bible its rightful place as the Word of God to the world. One Islamic writer says, 'There are many books in the world which are believed to be sacred. But except for the Quran, we do not find any religious book which thus projects itself as the word of God.'[5] However, a reading of the Old and New Testaments easily corrects this statement. As Dr Patrick Sookhdeo, a Christian scholar on Islam, has written, 'Islamic creed is in fact aimed at denying Christianity, especially the finality of Christ's ministry, death, suffering and resurrection, and asserting the supremacy of Islam.'[6]

By grace alone

The Quranic view of predestination is different from the Bible's. Islam believes, 'The omnipotence of God, mentioned in the Koran in countless passages, encompasses all areas and regions. God created the world, the animals, mankind, spirits, and angels, as well as the good and the bad. "Only that will happen to us, which God has ordained."'[7] The scriptural doctrine of election, however, is precious to those who believe (Rom. 9:7–13; Eph. 1:3–6). It is misunderstood when it appears to make God look like some fickle, selfish bully and when it clashes with the idea of free will. True freedom in the transformed life of a believer is the result of the free grace of God. The new birth brings forth the fruit of the Holy Spirit and is God's work in the soul. It is not through man's effort or sacraments (however defined) that we gain eternal life. The 'Five Pillars of Islam' are *de facto* Muslim sacraments; it is believed that fulfilment of them merits acceptance with Allah and the *Ummah* and provides hope in the Islamic system of salvation. However, 'The Five Pillars' remove the call to faith in Jesus Christ as the only Saviour of the world; salvation is wrongly believed to be found in obedience and fear alone. Believing in God's free grace is the hope found in the gospel. Christians say, along with the prophet Jonah, 'Salvation is of the LORD' (Jonah 2:9). Islam believes this of Allah but it has no place for the atoning work of Jesus Christ on the cross, by means of which God's grace flows to believers.

THE GIFT OF DIVINE GRACE UNTO SALVATION

Jesus Christ gives grace to God's people; this is something that Muhammad does not and cannot do. Muhammad was a great leader and a victorious general who converted people by the sword and demanded religious submission to Allah by the exercise of devotional works according to the 'Five Pillars of Islam', but only Jesus Christ can change the heart and wash away the sin of the soul.[8] This is why Christians, like Paul in 1 Corinthians 1, can speak of grace coming to them: 'Grace to you and peace from God our Father and the Lord Jesus Christ' (v. 3). This 'grace of God which was given to you by Christ Jesus' (v. 4) was given to the church through faith and made them spiritually rich, increasing their knowledge, assurance and hope. Grace is a gift flowing from God's effectual call: 'God is faithful, by whom you were called into the fellowship of His Son, Jesus Christ our Lord' (v. 9). Only God can give saving and sanctifying grace, and Paul acknowledges here that grace comes jointly 'from God our Father and the Lord Jesus Christ'. However, this gift of grace comes only through faith in the cross which Paul preached, which is foolishness to Islam: 'For the message of the cross is foolishness to those who are perishing, but to us who are being saved it is the power of God' (v. 18). Those who are called to salvation through the gospel of the cross of Jesus Christ are blessed indeed: 'Christ Jesus . . . became for us wisdom from God—and righteousness and sanctification and redemption' (v. 30).

Since Christ imparts wisdom that leads to righteousness and holiness with the cleansing and forgiveness of sins, the Christian cannot boast except in the Lord: 'Let him who glories glory in this, that he understands and knows Me, that I am the LORD' (Jer. 9:24). Paul was aware that this teaching was radical: that salvation is all of God's grace and not of man's works of merit or submission without grace, and it is always accompanied by the help of the Holy Spirit. 'These things we also speak, not in words which man's wisdom teaches but which the Holy Spirit teaches, comparing spiritual things with spiritual. But the natural man [the unsaved person] does not receive the things of the Spirit of God, for they are foolishness to him; nor can he know them, because they are spiritually discerned' (1 Cor. 2:13–14).

The subject of free grace is a recurring theme in the New Testament, and it is prominent also in the Old Testament: 'For by grace you have been saved through faith, and that not of yourselves; it is the gift of God, not of works, lest anyone should boast' (Eph. 2:8–9); 'Noah found grace in the eyes of the LORD' (Gen. 6:8). Now ascended and seated in heaven Jesus Christ is the giver of all saving grace: 'And of His fullness we have all received, and grace for grace. For the law was given through Moses, but grace and truth came through Jesus Christ' (John 1:16–17).

THE GIFT OF DIVINE WORDS UNTO SALVATION

Only when enlightened by the Spirit can we say that we are the real people (*Ummah*) of God. We could never have discovered the mysteries of God or the benefits of Christ's death by ourselves; we can know them only because they are revealed in the Word of God. Intellect and man's wisdom are not enough by themselves; therefore, divine help is required to see the path to eternal life: 'These things we also speak, not in words which man's wisdom teaches but which the Holy Spirit teaches' (1 Cor. 2:13). The Third Person of the Trinity understands the things of God because He is 'the Spirit who is from God' (2:12). Thus this epistle of 1 Corinthians is not written in words of Paul's own choosing or words dictated by man's wisdom. Rather, Paul used the very words which the Holy Spirit taught him to use (11:23a; 14:37). J. I. Packer says,

Revelation is a divine activity: not therefore, a human achievement. Revelation is not the same thing as discovery, or the dawning of insight, or the emerging of a bright idea. Revelation does not mean man finding God, but God finding man ... The fact we must face is that if there is no verbal revelation, there is no revelation at all.[9]

And so we believe that the actual words of Scripture (as found in the original autographs) were the very words of God, and that the Bible in its present form is entirely trustworthy because it has been kept intact, preserved by providence in the will of God. As we have noted, although this book is a response to Islam on the basis that the Quran, as we find it today, is the holy book of Muslims, we accept that the Quran was not always in its current form: 'It is certain that the Quran did not come together as a single volume in the lifetime of Muhammad. He made use of scribes to record some of his words in the Medina period, but most of his words were either memorized by his listeners or written down.'[10]

The Scriptures are all about what God has done for us through Jesus Christ: 'He [God] made Him [Jesus] who knew no sin to be sin for us, that we might become the righteousness of God in Him' (2 Cor. 5:21). God made Jesus Christ *sin for us* by laying on Him 'the iniquity of us all' (Isa. 53:6c). We have fallen into transgressions and turned to idols, 'every one, to his own way' (Isa. 53:6b). Robert Murray M'Cheyne said, 'God heaped upon His Son all our sins until there was nothing but sin to be seen. He appeared all sin; nothing of His own beauty appeared. Brethren, look at the love of Christ, that He should be willing to be made sin for us, and this was His love.'[11] In our unsaved state we feel no love for God, but He loves us with the very love which is His own essential nature, for 'God is love'. God's love requires that we respond to it with faith, repentance and trust.

Chapter 15

Staying true to the biblical Jesus

The challenge Islam presents us with, therefore, is to stay true to who Jesus Christ was in history and what He has done for us as revealed in the four Gospels, the epistles and the other books of the New Testament. Jesus Christ is the Citadel of the Christian faith, and staying true to Him is to witness to His love and resurrection. To hold fast to the divine revelation is to accept the dangers that accompany the proclamation of the gospel message in the face of Islam's progress. The words of Jesus to His disciples in John 15 make it clear that to be a Christian is dangerous: 'If the world hates you, you know that it hated Me before it hated you. If you were of the world, the world would love its own' (vv. 18–19a). Following Jesus Christ is a brave act of faith. Christians are to expect persecution—to live godly and to suffer! Islam has for the past fourteen centuries opposed and attempted to destroy public testimony and private witness to the true Prophet of God, Jesus Christ. However, believers are not alone and can expect help from the 'God of all comfort': 'Grace to you and peace from God our Father and the Lord Jesus Christ. Blessed be the God and Father of our Lord Jesus Christ, the Father of mercies and God of all comfort . . . For as the sufferings of Christ abound in us, so our consolation also abounds through Christ' (2 Cor. 1:2–3, 5).

Standing firm in the faith delivered by the apostles, evangelists and authors of the New Testament books is what is called for in the face of the challenge Islam brings to the Christian West and all the continents of the world. Islam challenges the integrity, authority, sufficiency and hope of the gospel. But the words of the Apostle Jude are meant for today as well as for the time when Gnosticism (in all its various forms), Arianism, Nestorianism, Modalism, and so on, and other heresies were abroad:

Beloved, while I was very diligent to write to you concerning our common salvation, I *found it necessary* to write to you exhorting you to contend earnestly for the faith which was once for all delivered to the saints. For certain men have crept in unnoticed, who long ago were marked out for this condemnation, ungodly men, who turn the grace of our God into lewdness and deny the only Lord God and our Lord Jesus Christ. (vv. 3–4, my emphasis)

The serious need to respond to this call from Jude is made clear by Patrick Sookhdeo in his book *The Death of Western Christianity*: 'Islam offers an attractive option for many people seeking purpose and meaning to life. Islam is based on three elements—all profoundly integral to the concept of identity—belief, belonging, and behaviour.'[12] His book is guaranteed to drive its readers to urgent prayer, because wisdom and grace are required from God to negotiate the present climate of opposition to biblical Christianity. Prayer for revival is urgently needed.

NOTES

1 Luke 17: 21, 'within you' is sometimes translated 'in your midst'; however, this cannot be the meaning here as Jesus makes it clear that the kingdom has two phases: one now and one to come. The first is at conversion (we are to pray, 'Your kingdom come', Matt. 6:10), the second at the Last Day and the Second Coming of Jesus (Matt. 25:34).

2 Tom Holland, *In the Shadow of the Sword* (London: Abacus, 2013), pp. 56, 59.

3 Patrick Sookhdeo, *Is the Muslim Isa the Biblical Jesus?* (McLean, VA: Isaac Publishing, 2012), p. 18.

4 Bruce Metzger, *The Text of the New Testament* (Oxford: Clarendon Press, 1968), pp. 34, 36–92.

5 Maulana Wahiduddin Khan, 'Introduction', in *The Quran: A New Translation*, ed. Farida Khanam (New Delhi: Goodword Books, 2009), p. xiii.

6 Patrick Sookhdeo, *The Challenge of Islam to the Church and Its Mission* (Pewsey: Isaac Publishing, 2009), p. 55.

7 Christine Schirrmacher, *The Islamic View of Major Christian Teachings* (Bonn: Culture and Science, 2008), p. 27.

8 It can be argued that the imperative to keep the 'Five Pillars' is a legalism that inspires fear, not love.

9 J. I. Packer, *God Has Spoken* (London: Hodder & Stoughton, 1985), pp. 46, 76.

10 Peter G. Riddell and Peter Cotterell, *Islam in Conflict: Past, Present and Future* (Leicester: IVP, 2003), p. 58.

11 Robert M. M'Cheyne, *God Made a Path*, ed. Stanley Barnes (Belfast: Ambassador, 1997), p. 103.

12 Patrick Sookhdeo, *The Death of Western Christianity* (McLean, VA: Isaac Publishing, 2017), p. 139.

The free offer of salvation

For I am not ashamed of the gospel of Christ, for it is the power of God to salvation for everyone who believes, for the Jew first and also for the Greek. For in it the righteousness of God is revealed from faith to faith; as it is written, 'The just shall live by faith.' (Rom. 1:16–17)

These words, with which we finish our 'engagement with Islam', express the faith of God's elect and the boldness which makes them living witnesses to the gospel of our Lord Jesus Christ. Salvation is grounded in the eternal love of God and it is given freely to all who believe in the resurrection of Jesus from the dead, for 'whoever calls on the name of the LORD shall be saved' (Rom. 10:13).

Adoption

The Bible teaches that the church is:

- *Universal in its extent:* it is worldwide in its scope and international in its coverage;
- *Local in its expression:* it is represented physically by local churches all over the globe;
- *Personal in its experience:* the church is not a denomination or an institution but is rather made up of those individuals who have been chosen of God, made living stones, a royal priesthood in order to offer up spiritual sacrifices to God through Jesus Christ (1 Peter 2:2–5, 9–10).

A Christian, then, is one who has God as his Father, and 'adoption is the ultimate experience because it brings us into the relationship of sonship'.[1] Following their justification by faith believing sinners are adopted into the family of God and cry out, 'Abba, Father' (Gal. 4:6–7). 'Adoption is the highest privilege that the Gospel offers; higher than justification ... because of the richer relationship with God it involves.'[2] This fellowship is the relationship John writes about in his first epistle: 'that which we have seen and heard we declare to you, that you also may have fellowship with us; and truly our fellowship is with the Father and with His Son Jesus Christ. And these things we write to you that your joy may be full' (1 John 1:3–4).

Included in the 'joy' is the love of God which has been shed abroad in our hearts by the Holy Spirit given to us on believing the gospel. 'The revelation to the believer that God is his Father is in a sense the climax of the Bible.'[3] Thus adoption has to do with redeeming love, joy and peace.

Salvation in Islam: the 'Eight Gates of Paradise'

While for Christians this adoption into God's family is a free gift of God's grace unto salvation, Islam is a system of works seeking eternal blessings from Allah by earning rewards through submission, fear and praise, whether by means of the 'Five Pillars of Islam' or through seeking to enter heaven through the 'Gates of Paradise'.[4]

Islamic tradition describes heaven as having eight 'doors' (called 'gates'). Some scholars interpret these doors (which were named by the prophet Muhammad) as being found inside heaven after one enters the main gate. Allah will admit into Paradise those who come through the gates: they 'shall not be open for those who reject Our signs and arrogantly spurned them: nor shall they enter Paradise until a camel shall pass through the eye of a needle. That is how We repay the evil-doers—Hell will be their bed, and over them will be coverings of fire' (Sura 7:40–41).[5]

The Eight Gates of Paradise, described in the Quran as 'The Gardens of eternity with gates thrown wide open to them [the righteous]' (Sura 38:50), are identified thus:
- Gate of Gnosis[6]
- Gate of worship (of Allah alone)
- Gate of prayer (*salah*)
- Gate of Jihad (holy war)[7]

• Gate of fasts (especially during Ramadan)
• Gate of charity (*sadaqah*)
• Gate of *hajj* (pilgrimage)
• Gate of mercy (forgiving others)

These 'gates' show 'where the core values of Islam lie. The names of the gates describe spiritual practices that Muslims strive to incorporate into their lives every day.'[8] It is said that

Paradise does not have only one gate, rather it has many gates. Allaah says (interpretation of the meaning):

'And those who kept their duty to their Lord (Al-Muttaqoon—the pious) will be led to Paradise in groups till when they reach it, and its gates will be opened (before their arrival for their reception) and its keepers will say: Salaamun 'Alaykum (peace be upon you)! You have done well, so enter here to abide therein.' (al-Zumar 39:73)[9]

The free gift of salvation

God always does what is right, just, proper, and consistent with all His other attributes. When we say that God *is* righteous, we mean that there is no wrong, dishonesty or unfairness in Him. When we say that God *does* righteousness, we mean, for example, that His method of justifying ungodly sinners is possible because Jesus, as our sinless Substitute, has satisfied all the claims of divine justice and love. His love provides what His righteousness demands—atonement for sin and forgiveness. God sent His Son to die as a Substitute for sinners, paying the penalty in full.

Jesus, thy blood and righteousness
My beauty are, my glorious dress . . .
Fully absolved through thee I am,
From sin and fear, from guilt and shame.
(Nicolaus Ludwig von Zinzendorf, 1739; tr. John Wesley)

Now that His justice is fully satisfied, God can righteously save all those who will take Christ as their Saviour by faith (1 John 1:9). As Paul wrote in Romans 1, 'For in [the gospel] the righteousness of God is revealed from faith to faith; as it is written, "The just shall live by faith"' (v. 17).

Paul is referring to God's way of justifying sinners by faith. Those who are not in themselves righteous are treated as if they are righteous when they believe. The expression 'from faith to faith' is a statement about the necessity of true faith to justify us in God's eyes; it says that the righteousness which is by faith is revealed to faith. Thus God's righteousness is not imputed (reckoned or declared) on the basis of works or made available to those who seek to earn or deserve it. It is instead a gift of God's free grace to all who believe the gospel: 'the gospel of Christ . . . is the power of God to salvation for everyone who believes' (v. 16). We need the gospel because we are lost eternally without its benefits, seeing that the wrath of God is revealed from heaven against the wickedness and unrighteousness of men (vv. 18–32).

God's abundant mercy

When Peter thought on God's abundant mercy towards repentant sinners he wrote, 'Blessed be the God and Father of our Lord Jesus Christ, who according to His abundant mercy has begotten us again to a living hope through the resurrection of Jesus Christ from the dead' (1 Peter 1:3). The word 'abundant' in common parlance means 'plenty', that is, 'copious amounts', 'ample sufficiency', a 'large quantity'. However, in New Testament Greek the original word is about quality as well as quantity. It is excessive and overflowing.[10] 'Abundant mercy' is translated as 'great mercy' in the NIV. This change of translation does not diminish the power of God's mercy on the individual, which is overwhelmingly subjective. What, then, is Peter saying? He is saying that he has received *much* mercy—vast and unending mercy—and that mercy from God is found in Jesus Christ his personal Saviour unto salvation. It is given to sinners and law-breakers, those who do not deserve it! This mercy is expressed thus by Paul: 'scarcely for a righteous man will one die; yet perhaps for a good man someone would even dare to die. But God demonstrates His own love toward us, in that while we were still sinners, Christ died for us' (Rom. 5:7–8). A fullness of divine love is expressed here.

The free offer of salvation

The sinner in Islam knows nothing of the free offer of forgiveness of his sins through atoning sacrifice: he has to earn mercy. Muslims' rejection of Jesus' atoning and reconciling work on the cross is grounded on their misunderstanding of the nature of God and His way of salvation through the blood of Jesus Christ, 'the Lamb of God'.

Through blood sacrifice God's people have always been able to approach the mercy seat and find forgiveness and the righteousness faith delivers. This is seen in the Old and New Testaments. Adam and Eve were the first to experience this, and Abel their son the first to believe it as the way to reconciliation with God (Heb. 11:4) when he built an altar and offered a lamb, while Cain his brother gave bloodless vegetables which were rejected by God (Gen. 4:4–5). Abraham went to Mount Moriah and took Isaac (as a sacrifice) with him to make an offering to God. Moses and the children of Israel escaped death when the death angel saw the blood of the Pascal lamb and passed over the Hebrew houses which had the blood of sacrifice on them (Exod. 12). Thus it was that the greatest Old Covenant prophet John the Baptist declared Jesus to be 'The Lamb of God who takes away the sin of the world' (John 1:29, 36). When Jesus came to earth it was as the One who 'must take the sinner's place, and bear sin's curse and pay sin's debt, and suffer sin's penalty and wash out sin's filth, and atone for sin's malignity'[11] (Isa. 53:4–6; 2 Cor. 5:20b–21).

Thus, acceptance with God which brings peace to the soul has been achieved through atoning sacrifice since the beginning of time. It has always been the way to find forgiveness and peace with God. Faith in the immutability of God's character leads us to believe that the principles by which He acted in the past are the same today under the New Covenant. Therefore, His method of dealing with His people is in a covenant relationship ratified by the blood of the everlasting covenant (Matt. 26:28; Mark 14:24; 1 Cor. 11:25; Heb. 7:22; 9:15; 12:24).

The true people of God

The writer of the First Epistle of John in the late first century (*c.* AD 96) laid before his readers at least *four marks* of the true people of God:

The *first mark* is a hatred of personal sin. This internal mark is the fruit of the new birth, or as John designates it, being 'born of God' (1 John 3:9). Some religions like to talk about the sins and transgressions of others but born-again saints mourn over their own sinful nature and failure not to sin (1 John 2:1b; Rom. 7:19). This mark is a witness that the new life of the Holy Spirit is indwelling the soul, giving a longing not to offend God by sinning.

The *second mark* is that forgiveness of sins is found and known through repentance and faith in the cross-work of Jesus Christ. This results in a lifting of the guilt and sin burden and brings a welcome assurance of peace in the soul. Those who are right with God possess a peace that passes all understanding. This is another subjective and experimental mark of conversion.

The *third mark* is the inner witness of God the Holy Spirit. As Paul describes it, 'The Spirit Himself bears witness with our spirit that we are children of God' (Rom. 8:16), while John speaks of the Christian's 'anointing which you have received from Him [and which] abides in you' (1 John 2: 20, 27a). The 'anointing' (Gk *charisma*) is the witness of the Holy Spirit in the believer. This is not a theory of initiation but rather a gift of conversion. As a result the Holy Spirit becomes the believer's comforter, guide, teacher and witness of the reality of conversion. In biblical language, believers have tasted that the Lord is gracious, for the Holy Spirit is the earnest or 'guarantee' of our inheritance: 'Having believed,' says Paul, 'you were sealed with the Holy Spirit of promise, who is the guarantee of our inheritance until the redemption of the purchased possession, to the praise of His glory' (Eph. 1:13–14). Other biblical texts agree:

It is the Spirit who bears witness. (1 John 5:6)

He who believes in the Son of God has the witness in himself. (1 John 5:10)

[God] has sealed us and given us the Spirit in our hearts as a guarantee. (2 Cor. 1:22)

The Holy Spirit also witnesses to us. (Heb. 10:15)

The *fourth mark* is the embracing of the truth as it is in Jesus Christ. This is an acceptance of the Bible's record of the life, witness and work of the historical Jesus. This truth has become known as the 'doctrine [or teaching] of Christ' (2 John 9). Who was Jesus and what has He done to merit the praise and worship Christians give to Him? His revealed divinity was a new and even blasphemous idea in first-century Palestine, and the idea that God had become man (so that the sons of men might become the sons of God) was extraordinary and dangerous! The doubting Apostle Thomas was slow to accept it (John 20:24–28) and the Athenians who heard it spoken of were reluctant too. Nevertheless, Paul 'preached to them Jesus and the resurrection. And they took him and brought him to the Areopagus, saying, "May we know what this new doctrine is of which you speak?"' (Acts 17:18–19).

Charles Wesley captures these proofs perfectly with his verse,

No man can truly say
That Jesus is the Lord,
Unless thou take the veil away,

Chapter 16

And breathe the living word;
Then, only then, we feel
Our interest in His blood,
And cry, with joy unspeakable:
'Thou art my Lord, my God!'
(Charles Wesley, 'Spirit of Faith, Come Down', 1746)

NOTES

1   Erroll Hulse, 'Recovering the Doctrine of Adoption', *Reformation Today* 105 (1988), p. 5.
2   J. I. Packer, 'Adoption', in *Knowing God* (London: Hodder & Stoughton, 1973), pp. 230–231.
3   Ibid., p. 225.
4   ' . . . If anyone makes the assistance of grace depend on the humility or obedience of man and does not agree that it is a gift of grace itself that we are obedient and humble, he contradicts the Apostle who says, "What have you that you did not receive?" (1 Cor. 4:7), and, "But by the grace of God I am what I am" (1 Cor. 15:10).' The Council of Orange, Canon 6.
5   Maulana Wahiduddin Khan, *The Quran: A New Translation*, ed. Farida Khanam (New Delhi: Goodword Books, 2009). The words 'the camel can pass through the eye of the needle' come from Matt. 19:24: 'I say to you, it is easier for a camel to go through the eye of a needle than for a rich man to enter the kingdom of God.'
6   'The Eight Gates of Paradise', Darvish, accessed 20 February 2018, https://darvish. wordpress.com/2008/01/03/the-eight-gates-of-paradise/.
7   'Note that the Quran calls upon Muslims to solve issues by peaceful means, and only engage in defensive battles: "Let there be no hostility except to those who practice oppression"' (Quran 2:193). However, the full verse seems to contradict this interpretation: 'Fight them until there is no more *fitna* [religious persecution] and religion belongs to God alone. If they desist, then *let there be no hostility, except towards aggressors*.' Khan, *The Quran*, p. 21.
8   Huda, 'Doors of Jannah: Islam's Eight Doors, or Gates, to Heaven', Learn Religions, accessed 20 February 2018, https://www.thoughtco.com/doors-of-jannah-2004342.
9   'A Christian Is Asking What Is Written on the Gate of Paradise', Islam Question & Answer, accessed 20 February 2018, https://islamqa.info/en/38161.
10 The Greek reads *to polu autou eleos*.
11 Henry Law, *The Gospel in Exodus* (London: Banner of Truth Trust, 1967), p. 15.

The Quran and creation

In the beginning God created the heavens and the earth. (Gen. 1:1)

The creation story with its different parts cannot be found in one place in the Quran but elements and comments from Muhammad are scattered throughout Islam's holy book. Thus we need to search widely to find the Islamic doctrine on creation and humanity's origins. With regard to the origins of the universe, some Muslims accept the view of long ages with its death and suffering in the evolution of man and beasts, while others reject evolution entirely, holding that there is incompatibility between Quranic teaching and Darwin's theory.[1] Western Islam wants to appear modern when it comes to science; however, it is inextricably bound to the text of the Quran, and this has led to mental gymnastics to keep in step with current evolutionary ideas, resulting in strange and contradictory explanations as to what the Quran means in the light of up-to-date interpretations of the beginning of human life and the age of the earth.

The Islamic view

CREATION OF THE WORLD

Islam teaches that all creation is from the hand of Allah. Allah created the heavens in six days, and he made the earth in two days and the sky from smoke/vapour. Thus it appears to support *creatio ex nihilo* (creation from nothing). The Quran says that Allah created the earth in 'two Days (periods) . . . He is the Lord of the universe. In two days He formed seven heavens . . . and adorned the lower heaven with brilliant lamps (stars) and guarded it' (Sura 41:9–12). He 'created the heavens and the earth in six Days (periods) then He ascended the Throne' (Sura 10:3; see also 7:54; 32:4; 57:4).

But not all Muslims hold to *creatio ex nihilo*. I. A. Ibrahim, commenting on Sura 41:11, says,

'Then He turned to the heavens when it was a vapour', indicating that the world was created out of 'smoke' or vapour: 'an opaque highly dense and hot gaseous composition' that originated from the Big Bang. Thus the heavens and earth were one connected entity [Sura 21:30]. Then out of this heterogeneous 'smoke' they were formed and separated from each other.[2]

Here Ibrahim is embracing a modern Big Bang cosmology and he seeks to justify the Quranic view of the universe's beginning by the observance of new stars forming out of the remnants of that 'smoke' as proof of its origin. However, the Quran's Sura 2:29 states, 'It is He who created everything on earth for you: then He turned towards heaven, and fashioned it into the seven heavens.' Here, Allah creates the earth first, then heaven!

Tradition dating back to Abd Allah ibn Abbas (born *c.* AD 619) states, quoting Muhammad,

God created the earth on Sunday and Monday. He created the mountains and the use they possess on Tuesday. On Wednesday He created the trees, water, cities and cultivated and barren land. These are four days … On Thursday He created the heaven. On Friday, He created the stars, the sun and the moon, and the angels; until three hours remained. In the first of these three hours, He created the terms (of human life), who would live and who would die. In the second, He cast harm upon everything that is useful for human kind, and in the third, (he created) Adam and had him dwell in Paradise (al-Tabari, 188).[3]

Muslims are taught that the creation itself is greater than the creation of man: 'Certainly, the creation of the heavens and the earth is greater than the creation of mankind' (Sura 40:57; cf. 79:27).

CREATION OF HUMANITY

There are various statements in the Quran about the creation of mankind which, if not contradictory, seem to be incompatible:

God created every creature from water. Some crawl upon their bellies, others walk on two legs and others on four. (Sura 24:45)

In the name of your Lord, who created: created man from a clot (of blood). (Sura 96:1–2)[4]

[God] created [Adam] from dust: then said to him, 'Be!' and he was. (Sura 3:58)

He has created you through different stages of existence . . . and caused you to grow. (Sura 71:14–17)

He [man] was created from spurting fluid, issuing from between the backbone and the breastbone [ribs]. (Sura 86:6–7)[5]

These references seem to indicate that Allah created life forms suddenly and perfectly from existing matter. Adam[6] had no parents and was created a fully formed human person. 'God then teaches Adam the names of all things and assembles the angels in front of Adam so as to show them . . . the high intellectual capacity of Adam':[7] 'And He taught Adam all the names, then He set them before the angels and said, "Tell Me of the names of these, if what you say be true"' (Sura 2:31). 'God later places Adam and Eve in the garden and tells them that they are free to enjoy of its fruits [but] not to come near a certain tree (2:35)'.[8]

Appendix 1

PARADISE

Adam and 'his wife'[9] were given Paradise to live in, which does not appear to have been on earth (Sura 2:35, 36b). Paradise was a garden of delights; there they were to 'eat and drink from wherever you wish, but do not approach this tree, lest you become wrongdoers' (Sura 7:19–25). The punishment for disregarding God's warning about Satan and eating the fruit of the forbidden tree meant that Adam and Eve became conscious of their nakedness and began to cover themselves with the leaves of the Garden. Satan caused Adam and his wife 'to slip', which 'brought about the loss of their former state', and they were put on the earth to live until they died (Sura 2:36).

In the Garden of Eden, Satan (often identified as Iblis) lures Adam and Eve into disobeying God by tasting the fruit from the forbidden tree. God sends Adam and Eve out into the rest of the earth . . .

According to the Quran, God had already decided before the creation of Adam that mankind (Adam and his progeny) would be placed on earth [Sura 15:19–20]. Islam does not describe mankind's life on earth as a punishment, rather as part of God's plan ['Have We not made the earth a receptacle for the living and the dead?', Sura 77:25–26].[10]

THE BOOK OF GENESIS REWRITTEN

This appears to be a rewriting of the account of the creation and fall of Adam and Eve in Genesis 3. From what we have seen, Muslims thus elevate the Garden of Eden up from earth and identify it with *jannah*, which means 'garden', the abode of the righteous (i.e. Paradise). This is where the righteous go when they die.[11] Thus when Adam (who was created righteous) and his wife (Hawa, the mother of mankind, equivalent to Eve, also created righteous) disobeyed Allah's instruction they were banished from Paradise down to earth, where mankind learned to live a righteous life (the Muslim way) and earn their path to Paradise. Allah does not live in Paradise—he is above it: being eternal he has no 'place'. Paradise is the kingdom Allah has created, and no one will disobey the Almighty's will. That is why Adam and Eve were banished from Paradise: they did what was inconceivable.[12]

PROCREATION

The Muslim author I. A. Ibrahim appears to see embryonic development:

We created man from the essence of clay, then We placed him as a drop of fluid in a safe place, then We developed that drop into a clinging form, and We developed that form into a lump of flesh, and We developed that lump into bones, and clothed the bones with flesh. Then We brought him into being as a new creation. (Sura 23:12–14)

Ibrahim argues that the growth of the embryo is described by the Arabic words used: *alaqah*, which describes a 'blood clot'—'the embryo at this stage is like a clot of blood'. The *alaqah* then becomes a *mudghah* ('chewed substance'), appearing at twenty-eight days old like a 'piece of gum that has been chewed' because the embryo 'somewhat resembles teeth marks in a chewed substance'. He concludes, 'These descriptions were revealed to Muhammad from God. He could not have known such details because he was an illiterate man with absolutely no scientific training.'[13] For I. A. Ibrahim, what was recorded in the seventh century AD is proof that the Quran is Allah's divine word to mankind and it must fit with modern evolutionary ideas.

The Quran describes the two sons of Adam and Eve, Cain (Qabil) and Abel (Habil), and their descendants as having an innate knowledge of God: 'God took all of Adam's progeny *from his back while they were still in heaven*. He asked each of them "am I not your Lord?"' (Sura 7:172, emphasis added). 'For this reason, it is believed that all humans are born with an innate knowledge of God.'[14] However, another English translation of Sura 7:172 uses the text of Hebrews 7:9–10 to adapt this idea to Western thought: 'When the Lord brought forth offspring from the loins of the children of Adam and made them bear witness about themselves, He said, "Am I not your Lord?"'[15] This raise a very important question for the reader of the English Quranic texts: are they accurately translated?

Conclusion

The Quran's perplexing statements on creation and humanity's origins contrast sharply with the biblical narratives on the creation in the first three chapters of the books of Genesis, the statements in Exodus (20:11) and various Psalms. Jesus Christ's testimony is that God 'who made them at the beginning "made them male and female"' (Matt. 19:4; Mark 10:6). The Islamic view presented in the Quran is fragmented, confusing and random while the Scriptures have a clear and detailed narrative and position on origins: 'The heavens declare the glory of God; and the firmament shows His handiwork' (Ps. 19:1).

When God created Adam and Eve, He placed them in Eden 'to tend and keep it' (Gen. 2:15). They were also told to 'fill the earth and subdue it' (1:28). This again contrasts sharply with the view that man was a mere chance happening. There is no hint in the Scriptures of Adam and Eve being ape-like creatures without souls who had evolved over millions of years. The opposite is true. They were farmers and shepherds who were commanded to 'be fruitful and multiply; fill the earth and subdue it; have dominion over . . . every living thing that moves on the earth' (Gen. 1:28).

The Bible's teaching that man is made in the image of God makes man special and unique, having a superior dignity and mind. Because of this humans can call God 'Father' and talk to Him in prayer, worshipping Him in Spirit and in truth (Luke 11:2; John 4:24). This sets man apart from the beasts not only anatomically and physiologically but also spiritually, allowing him to communicate with God through Jesus Christ.

Man's spiritual abilities are provided by his partaking of the 'divine nature' through faith (in the promises of the gospel, 2 Peter 1:3). God is Spirit (John 4:24), yet Adam (who was created from the dust of the ground) and Eve (who was created using a rib from Adam's side) were 'according to Our likeness', by which we understand that the Hebrew confirms that Adam was a created child of God. Adam and his descendants were made to have conscious spiritual fellowship with God (Rom. 1:2–21).

Adam and Eve were real historical people, and in the Gospel narratives of the New Testament and the epistles, they are regarded as such. Jesus Christ, His apostles and the other authors of the twenty-seven books teach that God created the world in six days and that the events of Genesis 1–11 are history. Jesus Christ Himself said that in 'the beginning [God] "made them male and female"' (Matt. 19:4–6). An unbiased reader of the Bible would agree that it leaves us in no doubt that Adam and Eve were regarded as historical people by Moses, who wrote the book of Genesis, by Jesus Christ and by the apostolic founders of Christianity. Nor is there any indication of any understanding other than that of six-day supernatural creation in the Scriptures of the Old and New Testaments.

An acceptance of evolution (whether in Christianity or Islam) may be an endeavour by some to remain in the mainstream of scientific thinking, but it has the effect of undermining the Scriptures as the inerrant Word of God, fully reliable in fact and doctrine.[16] Theistic Evolution refuses to accept the Bible's clear and timeless account of creation in six days by giving credence to scientific theories which are biblically absurd. If, when it comes to origins, the Bible cannot be trusted from the very first verse, how then can it be trusted when it comes to the great matters of the soul and eternal life? Is the onslaught of Islam against a biblical view an attempt to destroy the clear testimony of Scripture and keep its message from those whom Jesus Christ came to save?

Appendix 1

NOTES

1 Stephanie Hertzenberg, 'Are Islam and Evolution Compatible?', Beliefnet, accessed 23 April 2018, https://www.beliefnet.com/faiths/islam/are-islam-and-evolution-compatible.aspx.

2 I. A. Ibrahim, *A Brief Illustrated Guide to Understanding Islam* (Houston: Darussalam Publishers, 1996), p. 14.

3 *Encyclopedia of the Bible and Its Reception*, Vol 5 (Berlin: De Gruyter, 2012), pp. 998–999. 'Abū Jaʿfar Muḥammad ibn Jarīr al-Ṭabarī . . . (224–310 AH; 839–923 AD) was an influential Persian scholar, historian and xegete of the Qur'an . . . His most influential and best known works are his Qur'anic commentary known as *Tafsir al-Tabari* and his historical chronicle *Tarikh al-Rusul wa al-Muluk* (History of the Prophets and Kings), often referred to as *Tarikh al-Tabari*.' 'Al-Tabari', Wikipedia, accessed June 2019, https://en.wikipedia.org/wiki/Al-Tabari.

4 See *The Quran* (Rodwell edn, 1876), Sura 96, 'Thick Blood, or Clots of Blood', footnote 1, at https://www.sacred-texts.com/isl/qr/096.htm.

5 'Spurting fluid' here refers to seminal fluid, which the Arabs at the time believed originated from the backbone (or spine). This is also a clear scientific error as it is now well known that this is not the case.

6 The Hebrew *adam* [מָדָא] means 'red earth'.

7 'Adam in Islam', Wikipedia, https://en.wikipedia.org/wiki/Adam_in_Islam.

8 Ibid.

9 The Quran does not mention Eve by name!

10 'Adam in Islam'.

11 Paradise has seven levels according to Islamic teaching, as explained above.

12 'The Story of Adam and Eve', Masjid al-Muslimiin, https://www.almasjid.com/content/story_adam_and_eve.

13 Ibrahim, *A Brief Illustrated Guide*, p. 11.

14 'Adam in Islam'.

15 Maulana Wahiduddin Khan translation. Hebrews 7:9–10 reads, 'Even Levi, who receives tithes, paid tithes through Abraham, so to speak, for he was still in the loins of his father when Melchizedek met him.'

16 See The FIEC Statement of Faith, Article 2, 'The Bible'.

The names of Jesus[I]

Jesus was given names and titles, and the day will come when all of humanity will kneel before Him and acknowledge Him as 'Lord'. Here are some of His other titles, in the hope that people will look to Him and trust in His mercy.

Adam, the Last	1 Cor. 15:45
Advocate	1 John 2:1
Almighty	Rev. 1:8
Alpha & Omega	Rev. 1:8; 21:6
Amen	Rev. 3:14
Anchor	Heb. 6:18
Ancient of Days	Dan. 7:9–11 with Rev. 1:13–16
Anointed, His	Psalm 2:2; see also *Messiah*
Apostle	Heb. 3:1
Arm of the Lord	Isa. 53:1
Author	Heb. 12:2
Balm of Gilead	Jer. 8:22
Beginning	Col. 1:18
Beginning & the End	Rev. 1:8; 21:6; 22:13
Begotten, One and Only	John 3:16
Beloved	Eph. 1:6
Bishop of your souls	1 Peter 2:25
Branch	Isa. 11:1; Jer. 23:5; Zech. 3:8; 6:12
Bread	John 6:32, 33; 6:35
Bridegroom	Matt. 9:15; John 3:29; Rev. 21:9

Bright & Morning Star	See *Star*
Brightness of His (God's) glory	Heb. 1:3
Captain of their salvation	Heb. 2:10
Carpenter('s son)	Matt. 13:55; Mark 6:3
Chief (among ten thousand)	Song of Songs 5:10
Child (the young)	Isa. 9:6; Matt. 2:8–21
Chosen of God	Luke 23:35
Christ	Matt. 1:17; Mark 8:29; Luke 2:11; John 1:41; Rom. 1:16; 1 Cor. 1:23; 1 Peter 1:19; James 2:1; Heb. 9:24
Comforter	Isa. 61:2
Commander	Isa. 55:4
Companion of God	Zech. 13:7
Consolation of Israel	Luke 2:25
Cornerstone	Eph. 2:20; Isa. 28:16
Counsellor	Isa. 9:6; 40:13
Creator of all things	Col. 1:16

Appendix 2

Dayspring from on high	Luke 1:78	Great High Priest	Heb. 4:14
Day Star	2 Peter 1:19	Guide	Ps. 48:14
Deliverer	Rom. 11:26	Head (even Christ)	Eph. 4:15
Desire of all nations	Hag. 2:7	Heir of all things	Heb. 1:2
Door (of the sheepfold)	John 10:7, 9	Helper	Heb. 13:6
		Hiding Place	Isa. 32:2
End (see *Beginning & End*)	-	High Priest	Heb. 3:1; 7:1
End of the Law	Rom. 10:4	Holy Child	Acts 4:30
Express image of His (God's) person	Heb. 1:3	Holy One (& the Just)	Acts 2:27; 3:14
Faithful Witness	Rev. 1:5; 3:14; 19:11	Hope of Israel	Jer. 17:3
		Horn of Salvation	Ps. 18:2; Luke 1:69
Faithful & true	Rev. 19:11	I AM	John 8:24, 58
First & Last	Rev. 1:17	Image of (the invisible) God	Heb. 1:3; 2 Cor. 4:4; Col. 1:15
Firstborn from the dead	Rev. 1:5	Immanuel	Isa. 7:14; Matt. 1:23
Firstborn over all creation	Col. 1:15	Intercessor	Rom. 8:34; Heb. 7:25
		Jehovah	Isa. 26:4; 40:3
Firstfruits	1 Cor. 15:20, 23	Jesus	Matt. 1:21
Foundation	Isa. 28:16; 1 Cor. 3:11	Judge	Mic. 5:1; Acts 10:42
Fountain	Jer. 2:13; Zech. 13:1	Just One	Acts 7:52
Forerunner	Heb. 6:20	King	Zech. 14:16
Friend of sinners	Matt. 11:19; Luke 7:34	King of kings	1 Tim. 6:15; Rev. 17:14
Fullness of the Godhead	Col. 2:9	Lamb (of God)	John 1:29, 36; 1 Peter 1:19; Rev. 5:6, 12; 7:17
Gift of God	John 4:10; 2 Cor. 9:15	Last (see *First*)	Rev. 22:13
Glory of God	Isa. 60:1	Last Adam	1 Cor. 15:45
		Lawgiver	Isa. 33:22
God	John 1:1; Matt. 1:23; Rom. 9:5; 1 Tim. 3:16; Heb. 1:8	Life	John 11:25; 1 John 1:2
Good Teacher	Matt. 19:16	Light	John 12:35

Lion of the Tribe of Judah	Rev. 5:5		Rabbi	Matt. 26:25; John 3:2; 20:16
Lord	1 Cor. 12:3; 2 Peter 1:11		Ransom	1 Tim. 2:6
Lord of lords	1 Tim. 6:16; Rev. 17:14		Redeemer, Redemption	Isa. 59:20; 60:16; 1 Cor. 1:30
Man (see also *Son of Man*)	John 19:5; Acts 17:31; 1 Tim. 2:5		Refuge	Isa. 25:4
			Resurrection	John 11:25
Master	Matt. 8:19		Righteousness	Jer. 23:6; 33:16; 1 Cor. 1:30
Mediator	1 Tim. 2:5		Rock	1 Cor. 10:4
Merciful High Priest	Heb. 2:17		Rod	Isa. 11:1
Mercy Seat	Rom. 3:24, 25		Root	Rev. 22:16
Messiah	Dan. 9:25; John 1:41; 4:25		Rose of Sharon	Song of Songs 2:1
Mighty God	Isa. 9:6; cf. 10:21		Ruler	Matt. 2:6
Minister of the Sanctuary	Heb. 8:2		Sacrifice	Eph. 5:2
			Sanctification	1 Cor. 1:30
Nazarene	Mark 1:24		Saviour (of the world)	Luke 1:47; 2:11; 1 John 4:14
Offering	Eph. 2; Heb. 10:10			
Offspring of David	Rev. 22:16; see also *Root*		Second Man	1 Cor. 15:47
			Seed of Abraham	Gal. 3:16, 19
Omega	See Alpha & Omega		Servant	Isa. 42:1; 49:5–7; Matt. 12:18
One and Only Son	John 3:16			
Passover	1 Cor. 5:7		Shepherd	John 10:11, 14; 1 Peter 5:4
Peace, our	Eph. 2:14		Shiloh	Gen. 49:10
Physician	Matt. 9:12; Luke 4:23		Son	Isa. 9:6; John 5:20; 20:31; 2 Cor. 1:19; 1 John 4:14
Potentate	1 Tim. 6:15			
Prince of Life	Acts 3:15; 5:31		Son of Man	Matt. 9:6; 12:40; John 8:28; 13:31
Prince of Peace	Isa. 9:6			
Prophet	Acts 3:22, 23		Sower	Matt. 13:37
Propitiation	1 John 2:2; 4:10		Star	Num. 24:17; Rev. 22:11
Priest	Heb. 4:14		Stone	Ps. 118:22

Stumbling Stone	Rom. 9:33; 1 Peter 2:8	True Bread (see *Bread*)	–
Sun of Righteousness	Mal. 4:2	Truth	John 14:6
		Vine	John 15:1, 5
Teacher	Matt. 26:18; John 3:2; 11:28	Way	John 14:6
		Wonderful	Isa. 9:6
Testator	Heb. 9:15–17	Word	John 1:1

NOTES

1 Adapted from Ray Comfort, *The Evidence Bible* (2011), pp. 1689–1710. Used with permission by Bridge Logos, Inc. NKJV Complete Evidence Bible 9780882705255.

A harmony of Jesus Christ's appearances during the forty days between his resurrection and ascension (Acts 1:3)

No. and order	Person/people	N.T. text	Place, AD 30
1	To Mary Magdalene	Matt. 28:9 Mark 16:9 Luke 24:1–11 John 20:14–16	Jerusalem on the first day of the week, the Lord's Day
2	To the group of women who visited the sepulchre	Matt. 28:9 Mark 16:1–8	Jerusalem on the first day of the week, the Lord's Day
3	To the Apostle Simon Peter (Cephas) alone	Luke 24:34 (12) 1 Cor. 15:5a	Jerusalem on the first day of the week, the Lord's Day
4	To the two disciples on the Emmaus road (one was Cleopas)	Luke 24:13–31	Jerusalem on the first day of the week, the Lord's Day
5	To the apostles except Thomas with others	John 20:19 Luke 24:36–49 Mark 16:14ff.	Jerusalem on the first day of the week, the Lord's Day
6	To the apostles and Thomas (a week later)	John 20:26, 29	Jerusalem on the second Lord's Day (Sunday)
7	To the seven by the Sea of Tiberias (Galilee)	John 21:1–23	Galilee
8	To the eleven disciples on a mountain in Galilee	Matt. 28:16–20 1 Cor. 15:5b	Mountain in Galilee

Appendix 3

9	To more than 500 brothers at the same time	1 Cor. 15:6	Mountain in Galilee
10	To James, Jesus' brother	1 Cor. 15:7a	[Not known]
11	To the Eleven with others on Ascension Day	Acts 1:2–9 Mark 16:19f. Luke 24:51 1 Cor. 15:7b	Mount Olivet
12	To Paul 'as one born out of due time'	1 Cor. 15:8	Damascus Road

The Westminster Confession of Faith, Chapter 1: Of the Holy Scripture

Comments have been added in italics at key points below.

I. Although the light of nature, and the works of creation and providence, do so far manifest the goodness, wisdom, and power of God, as to leave men inexcusable; yet are they not sufficient to give that knowledge of God, and of his will, which is necessary unto salvation; therefore it pleased the Lord, at sundry times, and in divers manners, to reveal himself, and to declare that his will unto his Church; and afterwards for the better preserving and propagating of the truth, and for the more sure establishment and comfort of the Church against the corruption of the flesh, and the malice of Satan and of the world, to commit the same wholly unto writing; which maketh the Holy Scripture to be most necessary; those former ways of God's revealing his will unto his people being now ceased.

The London Baptist Confession of 1689 adds, 'The Holy Scripture is the only sufficient, certain, and infallible rule of all saving knowledge, faith, and obedience.'

II. Under the name of the Holy Scriptures, or the Word of God written, are now contained all the books of the Old and New Testaments [sixty six only]. All which are given by inspiration of God, to be the rule of faith and life.

The Bible is necessary because the light of nature and the works of creation

and providence are not sufficient to reveal the true nature and will of God or
to bring men to salvation through Jesus Christ (Heb. 1:1–2).

III. The books commonly called Apocrypha, not being of divine inspiration, are no part of the Canon of Scripture; and therefore are of no authority in the Church of God, nor to be any otherwise approved, or made use of, than other human writings.

IV. The authority of the Holy Scripture, for which it ought to be believed and obeyed, dependeth not upon the testimony of any man or Church, but wholly upon God (who is truth itself), the Author thereof; and therefore it is to be received, because it is the Word of God.

The Bible's authority is not dependent on the Church's testimony or dogmas
for its authority for it possesses an innate and unique authority all of its own
which is witnessed to by the Holy Spirit.

V. We may be moved and induced by the testimony of the Church to an high and reverent esteem of the holy Scripture; and the heavenliness of the matter, the efficacy of the doctrine, the majesty of the style, the consent of all the parts, the scope of the whole (which is to give all glory to God), the full discovery it makes of the only way of man's salvation, the many other incomparable excellencies, and the entire perfection thereof, are arguments whereby it doth abundantly evidence itself to be the Word of God; yet, notwithstanding, our full persuasion and assurance of the infallible truth and divine authority thereof, is from the inward work of the Holy Spirit, bearing witness by and with the Word in our hearts.

The Bible excels in truth, wisdom and light; however, it is the inward
illumination of the Spirit that seals its truth and authority by and with the
Word in our hearts.

VI. The whole counsel of God, concerning all things necessary for his own glory, man's salvation, faith, and life, is either expressly set down in Scripture, or by good and necessary consequence may be deduced from Scripture: unto which nothing at any time is to be added, whether by new revelations of the Spirit, or traditions of men. Nevertheless we acknowledge the inward illumination of the Spirit of God to be necessary for the saving understanding of such things as are revealed in the Word; and that there are some circumstances concerning the worship of God, and the government of the Church, common to human actions and societies, which are to be ordered by the light of nature and Christian prudence, according to the general rules of the Word, which are always to be observed.

The Scriptures as they now exist are sufficient to bring men to repentance and faith and must not be added to by new revelations of the Spirit, or traditions or works of men.

VII. All things in Scripture are not alike plain in themselves, nor alike clear unto all; yet those things which are necessary to be known, believed, and observed, for salvation, are so clearly propounded and opened in some place of Scripture or other, that not only the learned, but the unlearned, in a due use of the ordinary means, may attain unto a sufficient understanding of them.

The doctrine of perspicuity means that the Holy Scriptures are able to be understood by the learned and unlearned for salvation.

VIII. The Old Testament in Hebrew (which was the native language of the people of God of old), and the New Testament in Greek (which at the time of the writing of it was most generally known to the nations), being immediately inspired by God, and by his singular care and providence kept pure in all ages, are therefore authentical; so as in all controversies of religion the Church is finally to appeal unto them. But because these original tongues are not known to all the people of God who have right unto, and interest in, the Scriptures, and are commanded, in the fear of God, to read and search them, therefore they are to be translated into the language of every people unto which they come, that the Word of God dwelling plentifully in all, they may worship him in an acceptable manner, and, through patience and comfort of the Scriptures, may have hope.

The original autographs were immediately inspired by the Spirit of God so that they can be read in the vernacular for light and comfort and are meant to be the final arbitrator in all matters of religion.

IX. The infallible rule of interpretation of Scripture is the Scripture itself; and therefore, when there is a question about the true and full sense of any scripture (which is not manifold, but one), it may be searched and known by other places that speak more clearly.

X. The Supreme Judge, by which all controversies of religion are to be determined, and all decrees of councils, opinions of ancient writers, doctrines of men, and private spirits, are to be examined, and in whose sentence we are to rest, can be no other but the Holy Spirit speaking in the Scripture.

We understand and interpret Scripture by Scripture and it alone is the judge 'by which all controversies of religion are to be determined, and all decrees of councils, opinions of ancient writers, doctrines of men, and private spirits, are to be examined'.

Manuscript evidence for superior New Testament reliability, by Matt Slick (CARM)[1]

he New Testament is constantly under attack, and its reliability and accuracy are often contested by critics. If the critics want to disregard the New Testament, then they must also disregard other ancient writings by Plato, Aristotle, and Homer. This is because the New Testament documents are better-preserved and more numerous than any other ancient writings. Because they are so numerous, they can be cross checked for accuracy . . . and they are very consistent.

There are presently 5,686 Greek manuscripts in existence today for the New Testament.[2] If we were to compare the number of New Testament manuscripts to other ancient writings, we find that the New Testament manuscripts far outweigh the others in quantity.[3]

Author	Date Written	Earliest Copy	Approximate Time Span between original & copy	Number of Copies	Accuracy of Copies
Lucretius	died 55 or 53 BC		1100 yrs	2	—
Pliny	AD 61–113	AD 850	750 yrs	7	—
Plato	427–347 BC	AD 900	1200 yrs	7	—
Demosthenes	4th Cent. BC	AD 1100	800 yrs	8	—
Herodotus	480–425 BC	AD 900	1300 yrs	8	—

Suetonius	AD 75–160	AD 950	800 yrs	8	—
Thucydides	460–400 BC	AD 900	1300 yrs	8	—
Euripides	480–406 BC	AD 1100	1300 yrs	9	—
Aristophanes	450–385 BC	AD 900	1200	10	—
Caesar	100–44 BC	AD 900	1000	10	—
Livy	59 BC–AD 17	—	???	20	—
Tacitus	circa AD 100	AD 1100	1000 yrs	20	—
Aristotle	384–322 BC	AD 1100	1400	49	—
Sophocles	496–406 BC	AD 1000	1400 yrs	193	—
Homer (Iliad)	900 BC	400 BC	500 yrs	643	95%
New Testament	1st Cent. AD (AD 50–100)	2nd Cent. AD (c. AD 130f.)	less than 100 years	5600	99.5%

As you can see, there are thousands more New Testament Greek manuscripts than any other ancient writing. The internal consistency of the New Testament documents is about 99.5% textually pure. That is an amazing accuracy. In addition, there are over 19,000 copies in the Syriac, Latin, Coptic, and Aramaic languages. The total supporting New Testament manuscript base is over 24,000.

Almost all biblical scholars agree that the New Testament documents were all written before the close of the First Century. If Jesus was crucified in AD 30, then that means the entire New Testament was completed within 70 years. This is important because it means there were plenty of people around when the New Testament documents were penned—people who could have contested the writings. In other words, those who wrote the documents knew that if they were inaccurate, plenty of people would have pointed it out. But we have absolutely no ancient documents contemporary with the First Century that contest the New Testament texts.

Furthermore, another important aspect of this discussion is the fact that we have a fragment of the Gospel of John that dates back to around

29 years from the original writing (John Rylands Papyri AD 125). This is extremely close to the original writing date. This is simply unheard of in any other ancient writing, and it demonstrates that the Gospel of John is a First Century document.

Below is a chart with some of the oldest extant New Testament manuscripts compared to when they were originally penned. Compare these time spans with the next closest, which is Homer's *Iliad*, where the closest copy from the original is 500 years later. Undoubtedly, that period of time allows for more textual corruption in its transmission. How much less so for the New Testament documents?

Important Manuscript Papyri	Contents	Date Original Written	MSS Date	Approx. Time Span	Location
p52 (John Rylands Fragment)[4]	John 18:31–33, 37–38	circa AD 96	circa AD 125	29 yrs	John Rylands Library, Manchester, England
p46 (*Chester Beatty Papyrus*)	Rom. 5:17–6:3, 5–14; 8:15–25, 27–35; 10:1–11, 22, 24–33, 35; 16:1–23, 25–27; Heb.; 1 & 2 Cor.; Eph.; Gal.; Phil.; Col.; 1 Thess. 1:1, 9–10; 2:1–3; 5:5–9, 23–28	50s–70s	circa AD 200	Approx. 150 yrs	Chester Beatty Museum, Dublin & Ann Arbor, Michigan, University of Michigan library
p66 (*Bodmer Papyrus*)	John 1:1–6:11, 35–14:26; fragment of 14:29–21:9	70s	circa AD 200	Approx. 130 yrs	Cologne, Geneva
p67	Matt. 3:9, 15; 5:20–22, 25–28		circa AD 200	Approx. 130 yrs	Barcelona, Fundacion San Lucas Evangelista, P. Barc.1

Appendix 5

If the critics of the Bible dismiss the New Testament as reliable information, then they must also dismiss the reliability of the writings of Plato, Aristotle, Caesar, Homer, and the other authors mentioned in the chart at the beginning of the paper. On the other hand, if the critics acknowledge the historicity and writings of those other individuals, then they must also retain the historicity and writings of the New Testament authors; after all, the evidence for the New Testament's reliability is far greater than the others. The Christian has substantially superior criteria for affirming the New Testament documents than he does for any other ancient writing. It is good evidence on which to base the trust in the reliability of the New Testament.

NOTES

1 By Matt Slick, 'Manuscript Evidence for Superior New Testament Reliability', Christian Apologetics and Research Ministry (CARM), 12 October 2008, https://carm.org/manuscript-evidence.

2 Norman Geisler and Peter Bocchino, *Unshakeable Foundations* (Minneapolis, MN: Bethany House Publishers, 2001), p. 256.

3 The chart was adapted from three sources: 1) *Christian Apologetics*, by Norman Geisler, 1976, p. 307; 2) the article 'Archaeology and History attest to the Reliability of the Bible', by Richard M. Fales, PhD, in *The Evidence Bible*, Compiled by Ray Comfort, Bridge-Logos Publishers, Gainesville, FL, 2001, p. 163; and 3) *A Ready Defense*, by Josh Mcdowell, 1993, p. 45.

4 'Deissmann was convinced that p^{52} was written well within the reign of Hadrian (AD 117–38) and perhaps even during the time of Trajan (AD 98–117)' (Footnote #2 found on pg. 39 of *The Text of the New Testament*, by Bruce M. Metzger, 2nd Ed. 1968, Oxford University Press, NY, NY). Bruce Metzger has authored more than 50 books. He holds two Master's Degrees, a Ph.D. and has been awarded several honorary doctorates. 'He is past president of the Society of Biblical Literature, the International Society for New Testament Studies, and the North American Patristic Society.'—From *The Case for Christ*, by Lee Strobel, Zondervan Publishers, 1998, Grand Rapids, MI: pg. 57.

Islamic theology

Albirr Foundation UK, *Basic Principles of Islam* (London: Albirr Foundation UK, 2015).

———, *Salah: The Guide Book for Prayer* (London: Albirr Foundation UK, 2015).

Al-Masih, Abd, *Who Is Allah in Islam?* (Villach: Light of Life, 1985).

Barnabas Fund, *Unveiled: A Christian Study Guide to Islam* (McLean, VA: Isaac Publishing, 2011).

Burton, John, *An Introduction to the Hadith* (Edinburgh: Edinburgh University Press, 1994).

Copleston, F. S., *Christ or Mohammed?* (Harpenden: Islam's Challenge, 1989).

Deedat, Ahmed, *Is the Bible God's Word?* (Durban: Islamic Propagation Centre International, 1989).

———, *What Is the Sign of Jonah?* (Durban: Islamic Propagation Centre, 1976).

———, *What the Bible Says About Muhammad* (Birmingham: Islamic Propagation Centre International, 1989).

Gilchrist, John, *Christ in Islam and Christianity*, Qur'an and Bible Series No. 4 (Benoni, South Africa, 1985); at Answering Islam, https://www. answering-islam.org/Gilchrist/christ.html.

———, *Origins and Sources of the Gospel of Barnabas* (Sheffield: Fellowship of Faith for the Muslims Publications, 1992).

Hawting, Gerald, 'The Religion of Abraham and Islam', in M. Goodman, G. H. van Kooten and J. van Ruiten (eds.), *Abraham, the Nations, and the Hagarites* (Leiden: Brill, 2010), pp. 477–500.

Select bibliography

Khan, Maulana Wahiduddin, *The Quran: A New Translation*, ed. Farida Khanam (New Delhi: Goodword Books, 2009).

Masood, Steven, *The Bible and the Qur'an: A Question of Integrity* (Carlisle: Paternoster/Authentic Lifestyle, 2001).

Muhammad, Asad (trans.), *The Message of the Qur'an* (Bristol: Book Foundation, 2003).

Panosian, Edward M., *Islam and the Bible* (Greenville, SC: Ambassador Emerald International, 2003).

Riddell, Peter G., and Peter Cotterell, *Islam in Conflict: Past, Present and Future* (Leicester: IVP, 2003).

Schirrmacher, Christine, *The Islamic View of Major Christian Teachings* (Bonn: Culture and Science, 2008).

Solomon, Sam, *Not the Same God* (London: Wilberforce Publications, 2016).

Sookhdeo, Patrick, *The Challenge of Islam to the Church and Its Mission* (Pewsey: Isaac Publishing, 2009).

———, *Dawa: The Islamic Strategy for Reshaping the Modern World* (McLean, VA: Isaac Publishing, 2014).

———, *Is the Muslim Isa the Biblical Jesus?* (McLean, VA: Isaac Publishing, 2012).

———, *A Pocket Guide to Islam* (Fern, Ross-shire: Christian Focus / Isaac Publishing, 2010).

———, *Understanding Islamic Theology* (MacLean, VA: Isaac Publishing, 2103).

Zarabozo, Jamaal al-Din, *The Friday Prayer, Part 1: The Fiqh of the Friday*

Prayer (2nd edn; Ann Arbor, MI: Islamic Assembly of North America, 1998).

Zwemer, S. M., *The Moslem Doctrine of God* (American Tract Society, 1905; rep. Gerrards Cross: WEC Press, 1981).

Christian theology

Bayes, Jonathan F., *The Apostles' Creed* (Eugene, OR: Wipf & Stock, 2010).

Berkhof, Louis, *The History of Christian Doctrines* (London: Banner of Truth Trust, 1969).

———, *Summary of Christian Doctrine* (London: Banner of Truth Trust, 1968).

———, *Systematic Theology* (London: Banner of Truth Trust, 1971).

Bettenson, Henry, *Documents of the Christian Church* (London: Oxford University Press, 1974).

Calvin, John, *Commentaries: Ezekiel*, Vol. 21 (Grand Rapids, MI: Baker, 1979).

———, *Institutes of the Christian Religion* (Grand Rapids, MI: Associated Publishers and Authors Inc., [n. d.]).

Currid, John D., *Exodus*, Vol. 1 (Darlington: Evangelical Press, 2000).

———, *Genesis*, Vol. 1 (Darlington: Evangelical Press, 2003).

Dabney, R. L., *Systematic Theology* (Edinburgh: Banner of Truth Trust, 1996).

Dressler, H. H. P., 'The Sabbath in the Old Testament', in D. Carson (ed.), *From Sabbath to the Lord's Day: A Biblical, Historical and Theological Investigation* (Grand Rapids, MI: Zondervan, 1982).

Select bibliography

Edwards, Brian H., *Why 27?* (Darlington: Evangelical Press, 2007).

Edwards, Jonathan, 'The Perpetuity and Change of the Sabbath', *Works* (Edinburgh: Banner of Truth Trust, 1974).

Ferguson, Sinclair B., *John Owen on the Christian Life* (Edinburgh: Banner of Truth Trust, 1995).

Finlayson, R. A., *The Story of Theology* (London: Tyndale Press, 1969).

Geisler, Norman L. (ed.), *Inerrancy* (Grand Rapids, MI: Zondervan, 1982).

Harman, Allan, *Daniel* (Darlington: Evangelical Press, 2007).

Hastings, James (ed.), *The Greater Men and Women of the Bible*, Vol. 1 (Edinburgh: T&T Clark, 1938).

Hendriksen, William, *The Gospel of John* (London: Banner of Truth Trust, 1969).

Hodge, A. A., *Evangelical Theology* (Edinburgh: Banner of Truth Trust, 1976).

Hughes, P. E., *A Commentary on the Epistle to the Hebrews* (Grand Rapids, MI: Eerdmans, 1977).

Hulse, Erroll, 'Recovering the Doctrine of Adoption', *Reformation Today* 105 (1988).

Law, Henry, *The Gospel in Exodus* (London: Banner of Truth Trust, 1967).

Letham, Robert, *The Holy Trinity* (Phillipsburg, NJ: Presbyterian & Reformed, 2004).

Lloyd, Stephen, *Adam or Death* (Ely: Biblical Creation Trust, 2017).

Lloyd-Jones, D. M., *What Is an Evangelical?* (Edinburgh: Banner of Truth Trust, 1992).

McDonald, H. Dermot, *Who Is the Real Jesus?* (McLean, VA: Isaac Publishing, 2012).

McNaughton, Ian S., *Getting to Grips with Prayer* (Leominster: Day One, 2017).

————, *The Real Lord's Prayer* (Leominster: Day One, 2012).

Metzger, Bruce, *The Text of the New Testament* (Oxford: Clarendon Press, 1968).

Morris, Leon, *The Gospel According to John* (Grand Rapids, MI: Eerdmans, 1971).

Murray, John, *Redemption: Accomplished and Applied* (London: Banner of Truth Trust, 1961).

Packer, James I., *God Has Spoken: Revelation and the Bible* (London: Hodder & Stoughton, 1985).

————, *Knowing God* (London: Hodder & Stoughton, 1973).

Reymond, Robert L., *Systematic Theology* (Nashville: Thomas Nelson, 1998),

Ridderbos, Herman, *The Gospel of John* (Grand Rapids, MI: Eerdmans, 1992).

Schaeffer, Francis, *The Great Evangelical Disaster* (Eastbourne: Kingsway, 1984).

VanderKam, James C., *The Dead Sea Scrolls Today* (Grand Rapids, MI: Eerdmans, 1994).

Warfield, B. B., *The Inspiration and Authority of the Bible* (Phillipsburg, NJ: Presbyterian & Reformed, 1948).

———, 'Introduction to Francis R. Beattie's Apologetics', in *Selected Shorter Writings*, Vol. 2 (Phillipsburg, NJ: Presbyterian & Reformed, 1973).

———, *The Lord of Glory* (London: Evangelical Press, 1974).

Whitcross, John, *The Shorter Catechism Illustrated* (London: Banner of Truth Trust, 1968).

Whitefield, George, *Select Sermons* (London: Banner of Truth Trust, 1964).

Young, E. J., *Studies in Genesis One* (Phillipsburg, NJ: P&R, 1964).

———, *Thy Word Is Truth* (London: Banner of Truth Trust, 1972).

Bible history

Edersheim, Alfred, *Bible History* (Peabody, MA: Hendrickson, 1995).

Hodge, Bodie, *Tower of Babel* (Green Forest, AR: Master Books, 2013).

Holland, Tom, *In the Shadow of the Sword* (London: Abacus, 2013).

Sookhdeo, Patrick, *The Death of Western Christianity* (McLean, VA: Isaac Publishing, 2017).